The life story of DON BRADMAN

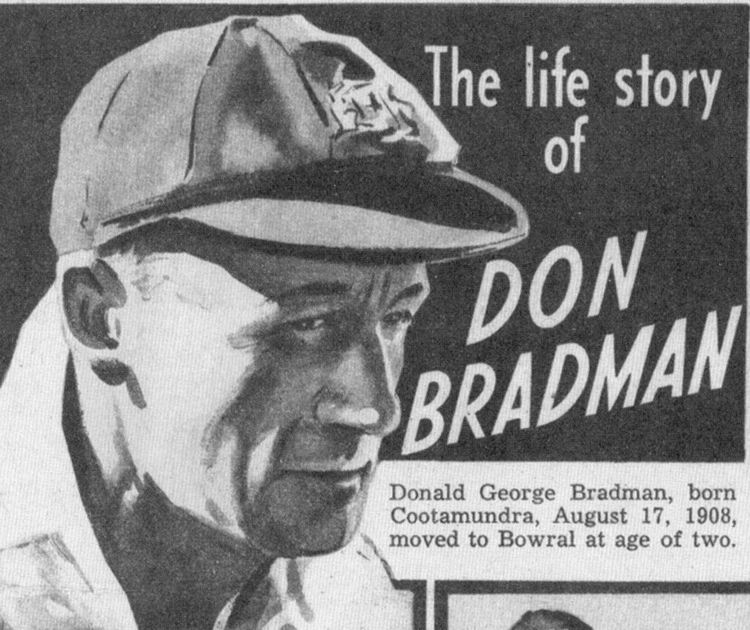

Donald George Bradman, born Cootamundra, August 17, 1908, moved to Bowral at age of two.

His first cricket bat was a tree branch and his wicket an old tank with a brick base.

He was too small for his first real bat. His father cut a few inches off the bottom.

At 12, he made his first century in a school match for Bowral against Mittagong.

At 17, he scored 234 for Bowral against Wingello. Later in same season he scored 300.

Next year (1926) NSW selectors called him to Sydney for a trial at the nets. He shaped well and was selected for State's Second XI that season.

About this time he nearly gave up cricket for tennis but in the end cricket won. Bradman never had cause to regret his decision.

Our Don Bradman

Happy Birthday, Dave

Love from the Moons

21/2/09

Our Don Bradman

Ken Piesse

ACKNOWLEDGEMENTS

The author would like to thank 'the voice of cricket', Richie Benaud, fellow Bradman Invincible Neil Harvey, that gentleman of cricket Brian Booth, and the often-called Bradman of Indian cricket, Sachin Tendulkar, for their Memories of the Don.

Thanks are also due to the following for their encouragement, guidance and assistance: Peter Allen, John Alverez, Ann Blair, Mark Browning, Colin Clowes, Charles Davis, David Frith, Alf James, Charles Leski, Marie Miller, Phil O'Meara, Geoff Poulter, Geoff Sando, Graham Smith, Phil Stelzer, Joel Williams, Bernard Whimpress, Ken Williams and Ken Wilson. And thanks also to Sydney's Mitchell Library for their assistance with the Bradman letters in their possession.

The majority of the pictures come from the Ken Piesse Collection. Others were supplied by: Peter Allen, pages 32, 49, 65, 96, 122, Australia Post, page 47, Australian Cricket Society, page 38, Ann Blair, page 168, Bradman Museum, page 107, 149, *Canberra Times*, page 110, Brian Clinton, front cover and pages 1, 170, Colin Clowes, Cricket NSW, page 33, *Cricketer* magazine, page 95, Patrick Eagar, pages 13, 101, Dean Golja, pages 92, 164, Brian Hansen, page 152, *The Herald & Weekly Times*, page 121, NSW Cricket Association, page 26, Phil O'Meara Collection, front cover, Megan Ponsford, page 46, Ken Rainsbury, front cover flap and page 82, Jim Rutherford, page 195, Graham Smith, page 116, *Sporting Life*, endpapers, St George Cricket Club, page 25, Joel Williams, front cover and pages 5, 9, 147, 188, Ken Wilson, pages 144, 149, 188.

Published by ABC Books for the
AUSTRALIAN BROADCASTING CORPORATION
GPO Box 9994 Sydney NSW 2001

First published August 2008

National Library of Australia
Cataloguing-in-Publication data
Piesse, Ken
Our Don Bradman: the greatest cricket story ever told
ISBN 978 0 7333 2366 9 (pbk.)
Bradman, Donald, Sir, 1908-2001
Cricket players – Australia – Biography.
Cricket captains – Australia – Biography.
Includes index.
796.358092

Cover, internal designs and typesetting by Helen Semmler
Editing by Neil Thomas
Text keyboarding by Kirby Jones
Colour reproduction and pre-press by PageSet
Project management by Richard Smart Publishing
Printed by SNP Leefung, China

54321

Contents

Memories of the Don
Richie Benaud • 7
Neil Harvey • 8
Brian Booth • 11
Sachin Tendulkar • 13
Introduction • 15
1 'Come on, Mum, come and have a bowl' • 19
2 Taming the Tiger • 23
3 A world to conquer • 27
4 'Our Don' • 31
5 'The boy wonder' • 35
6 'Bradman's tour' • 43
7 The darling of Australia • 49
8 Evil, insidious, brutal bodyline • 53
9 A mere mortal • 61
10 Captain of Australia • 65
11 1000 runs before the end of May • 71
12 Doing it for his son • 75
13 The Invincibles • 79
14 Cricket's ultimate matchwinner • 85
15 In love with Melbourne • 89
16 Jessie • 93
17 Life after cricket • 97
18 Interlude • 103
19 A heart of gold & other anecdotes • 111
20 Letters from the Don • 123
21 The Midas touch • 133
22 Ahead of his years • 145
23 Not everyone's cup of tea • 151
24 92...out • 165
25 The Don Declares • 171
26 Tributes, all • 177
27 How the Invincibles truly rate • 183
28 Collecting & the Don • 187
29 Don's team-mates • 195
30 An odd stat or two • 199
Further reading • 206
Index • 207

Richie Benaud

Memories of the Don

One of the things we know about Don Bradman is that he was the great entertainer in the batting department of the game. He filled grounds with paying spectators, many of whom went home when he was dismissed, often to the chagrin of his team-mates. This chagrin continued because although the Don was paid the same as all the other players in the team, or touring sides, he certainly made more money from endorsements and other outside interests than any of them - quite possibly more than the whole team put together. In 1930, after the Don made a triple-century at Headingley, Australian businessman Arthur Whitelaw presented him with a cheque for £1,000. In 2008 that would be worth around £45,000, so in the context of the 1930s and the Great Depression endorsements were enormous.

As a kid I loved the Dons' advertisement for Peter's Ice Cream with the old-fashioned cones (see page 144), and although he disliked Jack O'Hagan's foxtrot, *Our Don Bradman*, I always enjoyed hearing it on our old radio.

In 1930 Bradman did something you couldn't get away with nowadays. He was allowed to leave the ship in Fremantle (it was returning from his triumphs in England that year) for tours of honour in Adelaide, Melbourne and Sydney. His name was on clothing, cricket bats and other gear, and he had freelance jobs with Mick Simmons' sporting good stores, radio stations and newspapers.

Richie Benaud with the Don and Frank Worrell

I once saw a photograph of the 1930 Chevrolet that was custom-made for the Don and it struck an immediate chord. I was born in 1930 and that year my school-teacher father was posted to Koorawatha School in the south-west of New South Wales. For transport he and my mother bought a 1929 Chevrolet, a much-loved car with the number plate 136-819. It was almost the same car as the one the Don was given, but it certainly wasn't custom-made!

Neil Harvey

Memories of the Don

I was only eight years old when Don Bradman first became captain of Australia. He was everyone's hero, a fabulous cricketer, the all-time colossus of the game. Kids saying their prayers at night would often add at the end, 'And God bless Don Bradman'.

I was in awe of him, as was everyone else who loved the game. Never in my wildest dreams did I think I would get to meet let alone play with him. And I was to work alongside him, too, as an Australian selector. Talk about being blessed! We'd often nut teams out around the dinner table at his home in Kensington. And Jessie, his wife, was always a delight. Nothing was ever too much trouble. Both she and Don made you feel like you were family.

It remains one of my proudest, most cherished moments to have been the youngest member of Don's 1948 Invincibles. We were away for the best part of nine months and went undefeated in 34 matches. We won the Tests 4-0. We had a simply awesome team. I first met Don when I was named in an Australian XI which played the Indians in Sydney in late 1947. That was the game in which he made his 100th century. The reception when he ran a single for his 100th run was unforgettable. 'Nugget' (Keith) Miller was batting with him and came down and shook his hand. No Australian, before or since, has ever made as many 100s. It was a privilege being an onlooker; every eye was on him.

That was the summer I first broke into the Test team and got 153 in the final Test against India in Melbourne. It got me into the 1948 side and the tour of tours. I don't believe there's ever been a better cricket team or bunch of blokes. I learnt so much from them. We won four of the five Tests, the Manchester game being ruined by rain. As captain, Don was enormously busy. There was no support staff back then. He made speeches and then worked long into the night answering letters. It didn't matter who you were, he'd always reply.

England was still war ravaged in 1948 and so there were all sorts of restrictions in place. Don felt it important that he tour and help the game revive there. I was only 19 and it took me virtually all summer to get into the team. Early on I'd been a bit impetuous and was struggling to get amongst them, so I sent my roomie Sammy

Loxton to Don's room one night to ask what I should be doing. 'Go and tell your little mate,' said Don, 'if you keep the ball on the ground you can't get out.'

Sid Barnes had been injured in the draw at Manchester; he was walloped at short leg by the big Englishman Dick Pollard. I was included in his place at Leeds. What an introduction! What a match! I got 100 on my Ashes debut and we ran down 400 on a sixth-day wicket – there was no play on Sundays back then - and I was batting with Don when the winning runs were made. He and Arthur Morris had added 300 for the second wicket in one of the all-time great partnerships. They had a little luck here and there, but it was a marvellous effort on a tough wicket which at times turned square. Don made 173, one of the best and most timely of his 29 Test hundreds.

A few weeks later, at The Oval, we won the final Test by an innings, Ray Lindwall mowing through the Poms on the first morning. Only Len Hutton (30) made double figures. I don't think England has ever been dismissed for a lower score (52), not in a Ashes match anyway. Don batted for the last time on the Saturday afternoon, missed the first ball he faced and was bowled by the second, from Eric Hollies. Looking back on it I'm sure he was affected by the moment. The English captain Norman Yardley had set up a circle of honour around Don, and the Englishmen all doffed their caps when he called for three cheers. It was a tremendous gesture and one I know Don deeply appreciated.

That duck is probably the most famous one of all. It meant that Don's batting average 'fell' to 99.94. Sammy Loxton still loves to remind me that I'm the bloke responsible for Don not finishing with the perfect 100. 'Ninna,' he says, 'If you'd let Don hit that four at Leeds you would have changed history.' In fact, there was never any mention of such statistics. We had no idea that he was only four runs short of 7000 Test runs and an average of an even 100.

I love the story Arthur Morris tells about the Leeds game. He was at a business conference years later and someone referred to the duck. 'I do know about it,' said Arthur. 'I was there.'

'What were you doing? Business? Holidays?'

'Actually, I was up the other end.'

'Did you score any?'

'Yes I did…196!'

Youngsters today must blink with astonishment when they read that Don's batting average is almost forty runs ahead of the next best; it simply proves just how great a player he was. I didn't see him bat in the 1930s, but those who did said he was extraordinarily good. I thought he was an absolutely marvellous player in 1948 so he must have been out of this world before then. You felt so secure having him at the other end.

Don's contribution to the game continued for years after he retired in 1949. He was on just about every important cricket committee in Adelaide and at Australian Board level. His influence was enormous, even as a non-selector - he urged the selection of the young David Hookes for the 1977 Centenary Test. Hookes had made five 100s in six innings and was just the sort of player to excite the crowds. From 1966, I joined Don as a Test selector and really got to know him. 'The King' Jack Ryder was also on the panel. Two more knowledgeable blokes about the game you couldn't find. When Jack retired, Sam Loxton stepped in and we picked Dennis Lillee for the first time. During the 1970-71 Test series in Australia Englishman John Snow had been giving our batsmen curry and Don asked if we'd seen anyone who could return some of his fire.

'As a matter of fact we have,' we said. 'His name is Dennis Lillee and he comes from Perth.'

Don hadn't seen him bowl as Dennis had only played a handful of games in the West.

'Does he know where they're going?'

'No, but that's not necessarily a bad thing.'

'Okay...pencil him in.' (Dennis took 5-84 in England's first innings of the Sixth Test in Adelaide.)

As I got to know Don more it became clear that he was a truly great man. He had a tremendous influence on me, and in his centenary year I'm proud to have been one of 'his' boys.

Brian Booth

Memories of the Don

It is a particular delight to share some personal thoughts and reflections on Don Bradman during his centenary year. I hope they in a small way add to the passion and expertise Ken Piesse shows in this most alluring book.

Although I didn't see the Don bat, he had considerable influence on my life and cricket. While a youngster growing up in the small village of Perthville, ten kilometers south-west of Bathurst in country New South Wales, a day rarely passed without some reference to him. My Father, Snowy, was an ardent cricket lover who lived through the tough times of World War One, the Depression years of the early 1930s, and then World War Two. And through his extraordinary batting performances Don Bradman lifted the spirit of my father and his generation. He was their hero, and so he became mine as well. In our small kitchen hung two photographs, one was the Don and the other Stan McCabe. My father often called them 'the two greatest living batsmen'.

As a schoolboy playing backyard 'Tests' I imagined I was Don Bradman. It was always Australia versus England; I can't remember England winning once! I'd try and emulate his style, how he used to play one just in front of square to quickly get off the mark.

My secondary schooling started in 1946 at Bathurst High. My first cricket team was the Under 13a XI and I was captain I eagerly read every cricket book I found, savouring the descriptions of Don's magnificent pre-war performances in England, against the touring Englishmen in 1946-47, and then in England in 1948.

I was also considerably influenced by the sporting way the Don played the game. Consider the way he responded after being dismissed second ball in his last Test innings in 1948. On realising he had been bowled by leg-spinner Eric Hollies, he simply lifted his head, turned, gave a smile and walked quickly away from the wicket. I read that when he got back to the dressing-room he offered no excuse, merely saying 'fancy doing that!' It was an approach considerately different from numerous current-day players. Being 'professional' is no excuse. After all, cricket is still a game.

In 1952, I moved to Sydney to train as a physical education teacher at Sydney

Teachers' College. I tried out for the St. George District Cricket Club at Hurstville Oval and was selected for the first grade team, a position I held until my retirement in 1973. One of my team-mates was that marvellous left-handed opening batsman Arthur Morris, a member of Don Bradman's 1948 Invincibles.

Although I knew a great deal about Don Bradman, it was not until December 1955 that I met him. The occasion was my first Sheffield Shield visit to the beautiful Adelaide Oval. New South Wales was playing South Australia and Keith Miller was our captain. NSW won in three days and so on the following free morning Warren Saunders, my St. George club-mate, and I played a few sets of tennis on one of the grass courts at the rear of the Members' Stand. We noticed the Don walking along the adjacent path, and our match immediately increased in intensity. He stopped and watched for a few minutes before saying, 'Seeing how you two fellows batted in this match (in a score of 9-433 declared Warren made 23 and me just 9) I'd have thought you'd be better off practicing your batting rather than playing tennis!' And on he walked. Eight years later I made my highest Test score, 169, against South Africa at the 'Gabba. What a thrill when the Don came into the Australian dressing-room to pass on his congratulations. His comment, as at the tennis, was very much to the point. 'Congratulations, Brian. That's the best innings I've seen you play.'

Like many thousands of cricket lovers, I wrote to the Don on a number of matters. Two letters in particular mean a great deal to me. The first was when I was appointed captain of Australia for the First Test against England at the 'Gabba in 1965. In his letter the Don congratulated me on the honour and wished me and the team well.

The second letter arrived after the Third Test of that series in Sydney when I was again captain. Australia had suffered a heavy defeat and I was excluded for the next Test in Adelaide. The Don wrote: 'Never before have I written to a player to express my regret at his omission from an Australian XI. In your case I am making an exception because I want you to know how much my colleagues and I disliked having to make this move.' He wished me well, thanked me for my contribution to Australian cricket, and hoped I would soon return to my best form.

Both these letters indicated to me the Don's compassion, empathy and sincerity, and are still of considerable encouragement. As you can tell, I hold him in the highest regard. The Don made a significant contribution to Australian sporting, cultural and social history. He was a wonderful ambassador for cricket and the nation itself.

Brian Booth

Sachin Tendulkar

Memories of the Don

Meeting Sir Donald Bradman in 1998 on his 90th birthday was the greatest day of my life.

Along with Shane Warne and my great friend and manager, Mark Mascarenhas, we had a golden hour with cricket's all-time master, time that has lived with me ever since. Ten years later, in 2008, I was very proud to make Test hundreds at his old home grounds in Sydney and Adelaide. They were particularly special because they were almost certainly my last opportunities to play at those two magnificent grounds.

Although the Don never played in India he is a legend back there. In my country, where cricket is king, every little boy wants to be just like him.

It doesn't seem ten years since we met. On that unforgettable August day the Don made me feel so at ease. He talked about my batting grip and stance, and how they allow me to play shots all around the wicket. He was surprised to learn that I had been coached; he said I played with rare freedom, which delighted him. I think I was too nervous to say much. It was such an honour and privilege just to be there watching as he demonstrated how he used to play some of his shots. He told me how he'd liked to use a light bat because it allowed him to play a wider range of shots.

I wish I could recall every detail of our conversation. But I'll never ever forget the warmth and generosity he showed me. May he be just as big a name in cricket in 100 years time as he is right now, the centenary of his birth. Thank you, Ken Piesse, for the opportunity to contribute to this celebratory book.

Don Bradman

Introduction

Don Bradman was Australia's sporting colossus throughout the 1930s, the eighth wonder of the world and the ultimate idol for a nation ravaged by the Great Depression and on the verge of war. The finest batsman of his, or any era, the Don's freakish run of scores attracted phenomenal interest and raised spirits amid the gloom of food rationing and appalling unemployment. So huge was the crowd during a Sydney club game at Birchgrove Oval one Saturday that instead of fighting his way through the masses to the pavilion to have a cup of tea with his St George teammates, Bradman opted to spend the interval in mid-pitch and was mobbed, with the crowd invading the ground seeking autographs and wanting to shake his hand. 'I'll be Bradman and you can be all the rest,' was the common catchcry of thousands in backstreet and playground matches around the country.

Bradman scored more than 50,000 runs in an unprecedented streak of staggering scores. Included was 212 centuries, 117 of them in first-class cricket and 29 in Tests. He played his first competitive match at twelve and his last at 54.

His monumental 452 not out for New South Wales at the Sydney Cricket Ground in 1929-30 remained a world record for nearly 30 years. He was chaired from the ground by the very bowlers he had battered. In England in 1930, on the first of his four triumphant Ashes trips, his 974 runs in five Tests created a new Ashes high, eclipsing Walter Hammond's mighty 905 set just eighteen months earlier in Australia. It inspired the term 'Bradmanesque'.

Small at just 170 cm and slightly built at 65 kg, Bradman became Australian cricket's single most potent force. His awesome 334 in the Leeds Test of 1930 was to go unsurpassed among Australians at Test level for almost 75 years. He was all but unstoppable, relentless, focused and durable and no

At the Adelaide Test, 1928-29, 20 years old

bowler, or captain, seemed to have a conventional answer to his devastating efficiency. Such was his astonishing success that he was always expected to score heavily. Offices around Melbourne and Sydney would invariably empty around lunchtime if it was known the Don was 'in'.

Bradman Invincible Bill Brown loved to tell the story of the Sydney Cricket Ground crowd clapping ever-so-generously one day as he was walking off. 'I thought to myself, "That's very nice" then I realised they were clapping because I was out…guess who was coming through the gate…Don!'

Another of Bradman's contemporaries, Jack Fingleton, said it was usual to see thousands leave the ground when Bradman was dismissed. 'The atmosphere and much of the interest in the game walked back with Bradman to the pavilion. He was responsible for a great percentage of the enormous public interest in cricket between the two wars.'

Bradman's scoring was so spectacular and so consistent that 'BRADMAN FAILS' was a banner headline on Fleet Street one afternoon. He'd made 80! When he edged Maurice Tate to George Duckworth to end his monumental 334 during his superlative 1930 tour, one London billboard simply read 'HE'S OUT'. The Don was so famous that he did not need to be named.

After being invalided out of the Army in June 1941 with fibrositis, he was reluctant to play again, but changed his mind after his wife, Jessie, said it would be a shame if their young son, John, was denied the opportunity to see him play. He wanted, too, to help cricket become established again after seven dark years of the Second World War.

Having led the 1948 Australians undefeated in a triumphant English farewell, the Don was knighted and began his second phase in cricket as an administrator and selector; his stamina was to be just as enormous and influence vast.

In 1947 Bowral's Glebe Park was renamed Bradman Oval and in 1976 a match was played as part of a re-dedication ceremony between local and NSW players. Fellow NSW country legend Bill O'Reilly launched the match by bowling the first ball. It was directed wide down the leg side and the Don missed it.

He'd retired as a Test selector in 1971 and stood down from his last committee responsibilities with the South Australian Cricket Association in 1985.

Bradman's death, in February 2001, aged 92, came as a genuine shock and triggered front-page tributes worldwide. If anyone was going to live to 100, we thought it was going to be Don. He was truly Australia's bestknown son, a miracle in flannels.

Our Don Bradman, published to commemorate the centenary of his birth, will remind cricket lovers of the Don's greatest deeds in words and pictures. Many of the illustrations are little known or are being published in colour for the first time.

My thanks to the book's designer Helen Semmler for taking my very large portfolio of pictures and text and turning it all into such a readable book, and to everyone at the ABC, especially Richard Smart, for sharing in the Don's centenary celebrations.

Ken Piesse

CHAPTER ONE

'Come on, Mum, come and have a bowl'

He may have been only pint-sized but he had rare love of sport and the eye of an eagle.

Donald George Bradman was born at 89 Adams Street, Cootamundra in the sheep and wheat country of south-east New South Wales on 27 August 1908, the year in which English cricket's bestknown player, Dr W. G. Grace, made his last major appearance.

The youngest in a family of five, Bradman was two when his family moved in 1911 to Bowral, 100 km from Sydney in the southern highlands. There his father, George, started work as a carpenter. Though he was only small in stature, Don was an able sportsman from an early age. His first cricket games were played in the backyard of the family's small weatherboard bungalow in Shepherd St where he set up an old kerosene tin as a wicket. His mother, Emily, encouraged her enthusiastic son and often played cricket with him. Young Don would dash home from school and yell: 'Come on, Mum, come and have a bowl!' without waiting for afternoon tea, whereupon Emily Bradman would happily roll up her sleeves and commence bowling her best left-arm slows.

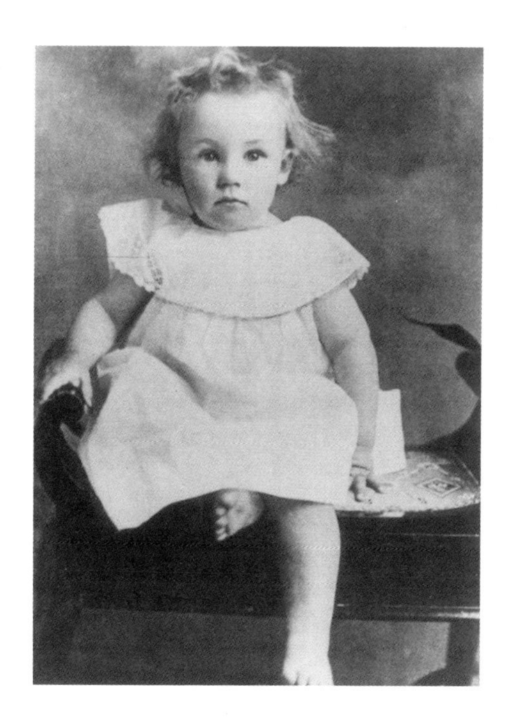

Unmistakably the Don - just look at the eyes

Young Don's passion and focus for the game was extraordinary, his reflexes honed by throwing a golf ball against the brick base of an old water tank a few metres away before hitting it on the rebound with a cricket stump. The ball bounced back at different speeds and

different heights and to even hit it required intense focus and co-ordination.

His natural ability had been immediately spotted by his father and uncles, George and Richard Whatman, who were champion bush cricketers. Besides playing cricket, Don excelled at tennis and rugby, was a fine schoolboy runner and in his mid-teens even defeated the table tennis champion of the southern highlands. But cricket was always his first love.

Like many country children, Don would be up at first light to help with the chores, but as soon as they were completed, back he would go to the old water tank, cricket stump in hand, for more practice. He was not satisfied until he could strike the rebounding ball at least three times out of four. To be successful, the exercise demanded a nimble brain, perfect judgment, quick feet and infinite patience.

He also improved his throwing and catching skills by aiming a golf or a tennis ball from varying distances at the lower rail of the wooden paling fence in his yard. The ball would rebound, whistling off the rail at all angles. If it was within diving reach, he'd propel himself sideways, to his left or his right. Rarely did he drop one. If

OPPOSITE BELOW: The Cootamundra, NSW, cottage where the Don lived until he was 18 months old

The water tank practise routine

the ball flew wide, he'd chase it down and send back his return low and hard at a fence post, always at bail height, pretending it was a set of stumps.

The schoolboy's zest for cricket and devotion to the skills of the game were soon to pay off handsomely. His father worked for the town builder, Alf Stephens, who doubled as the local mayor and captain of Bowral Town's XI. The team needed a scorer and Don was ideal. He would come dressed in neatly-pressed white shirt and shorts, in case there was an eleventh-hour withdrawal. One day a team member failed to turn up and Don took his place. In his short pants and gripping a bat that was far too big for him, he made 37 not out at Moss Vale. The young champ was away.

THE DON'S INTERMEDIATE SCHOOL RESULTS

Bowral High School, 1922

Art	B
Chemistry	B
English	B
French	A
History	B
Mathematics I	A
Mathematics II	B
Woodwork	B

Yours Truly
Don Bradman

CHAPTER TWO

Taming the Tiger

Few were fast-tracked like Don Bradman. Just six months before his first-class debut in Adelaide he'd been playing bush cricket with Bowral Town...

The boy Bradman came from the humblest of beginnings and had had no formal coaching when he amassed the first of several astonishing double and triple-centuries for Bowral Town. The most fabled of his youthful triumphs came at the age of seventeen when he was matched by champion leg-spinner-to-be, twenty-year-old W. J. 'Bill' O'Reilly from Wingello.

'The Tiger', Bill O'Reilly

Batting all afternoon, Bradman scored 234 not out. His last 50 included four sixes and six fours. His massive score prompted headlines in five local newspapers and even warranted a mention in a Sydney newspaper. This performance was the first real sign of Don's extraordinary thirst for runs.

'Even though his size suggested that he would have been better fitted physically to have been riding at Randwick, he summoned the energy required to land the ball right over the fence on half a dozen occasions,' said O'Reilly years later in his book *Tiger: Sixty Years in Cricket*. 'One wondered where he was hiding the battery that generated the power.'

In the grand final that season, Bradman scored an even 300 and shared in a second-wicket stand of 374 with his uncle George Whatman, who made 227. The game went five consecutive Saturdays into early June, Bowral Town winning by an innings and 338 runs. In all matches that season, the Don aggregated 1381 runs and

Back in Bowral with Alf Stephens, captain of Bowral Town's XI when Don played as a schoolboy

OPPOSITE: Don in the St George cap

averaged in excess of 100 runs per innings. He also took 51 wickets at 7.8 with his leg-breaks and held 26 catches. The boy was performing in a fashion which astonished even his mother and father.

The following spring, Bradman sampled turf cricket for the first time, representing Southern Districts at Sydney Country Week. At the carnival's conclusion he made 98 for Country v City at the Sydney Cricket Ground. His hero, Charlie Macartney, scored a century in the same game. Years earlier, in 1920-21, a young Don had attended the Sydney Test match with his father and watched in awe as Macartney dominated the English bowling with a scintillating array of shots. 'I shall not be satisfied until I play on this ground,' Bradman told his father.

His progress had been emphatic ever since his invitation to trial in the city at the summer start. And he finished on a high, too, with another triple-century, not out, as Bowral Town won another premiership. The New South Wales XI had been depleted by retirement and the unavailability of many of the '26 Ashes team who were not due to arrive back in Australia until after NSW's opening fixture in Brisbane. A. G. 'Johnnie' Moyes was part of the selection panel enlisted to replenish the side, particularly the bowlers and Bradman was among several of the invitees from the immediate country areas — as much for his leg-breaks as for his batting skill. 'The youngster looked a batsman,' said Moyes, a former first-class representative. 'He had a quick eye and speedy footwork... though no-one could have imagined what power was latent in the small frame. It was a severe trial, yet young Don faced it without any outward sign of nerves, in spite of the fact that he must have realised that he had come to the crossroads of his career.' Also in the crowd watching the youngsters try out were ex-internationals Harry Donnan and C.T. B. 'Terror' Turner, one of Australia's greatest early Ashes legends.

Although Bradman's junior cricket had been played almost exclusively on concrete wickets covered with coir matting, he immediately adjusted to the faster grass surfaces, impressing as a young player of the future, his repertoire of shots stretching all around the wicket. He was cool and played the ball 'late', a trademark of a quality batsman.

He was invited to join the St George first-grade team and on debut scored an even-time century at Petersham. Many more were now taking notice of the quiet young man with the ready smile and the trousers which stopped an inch or two short of his boots. His potential seemed limitless.

HAPPY MEMORIES

'In that memorable Test match I was privileged to see (Charles) Macartney in all his glory making 170. I can picture his delicate leg glances and one flashing drive, not through the covers but over the top. My great favourite was Johnnie Taylor. He was my boyhood hero, though I never met him, and I can still remember the sinking feeling which came over me when Patsy Hendren caught him out'

Bradman, aged twelve, on his first trip to the Sydney Cricket Ground.

CHAPTER THREE

A world to conquer

Bright eyed and with the sunniest of smiles, a young Don Bradman had uncanny ability and rare self-belief...

Having averaged almost 50 in his debut season of Sydney grade cricket, a teenage Don Bradman was elevated into the NSW XII for the first time for the team's southern tour in December 1927, when Charlie Macartney retired and Test pair Jack Gregory and H. 'Hammy' Love withdrew. It had been a meteoric rise. On the eve of selection the teenager had made a polished 130 not out against a Paddington attack which included expressman Gregory. Just over six months earlier he'd been playing in the bush.

The NSW team travelled from Sydney's Central Station to Adelaide, taking advantage of the new railway link, and stopped off for a match at Broken Hill. Playing in street shoes on a concrete wicket, Bradman made 46 before being stumped. He shared in a near 100-run stand with his captain Alan Kippax.

They were timely runs as he was selected to replace Archie Jackson, who was indisposed.

The South Australians included the wily spin bowler Clarrie Grimmett, and batting at No.7 Bradman announced himself emphatically with a memorable century in searing heat and despite the inconvenience of a sore finger. He didn't give even one chance. Few as unfledged had ever advanced as confidently at Grimmett.

OPPOSITE: the Don in NSW colours for the first time, Adelaide, 1927-28. Back row, left to right, Norbert Phillips, Frank Jordan, Albert Scanes, Sam Everett, Tommy Andrews, the Don, Archie Jackson, Bert Oldfield. Front, Gordon Morgan, Alan Kippax (captain), Dr F. V. McAdam (manager), Ray MacNamee, Arthur Mailey

Young Sydney starlets: the Don with Archie Jackson who died tragically young in 1933

THE DON

Don Bradman was first called 'The Don' in a Sydney newspaper after making a century on debut against Clarrie Grimmett and Co. in Adelaide.

He seemed to skip metres out of his crease when driving down the ground. His first 50 came in just over an hour.

Watching from the side-on from the pavilion, the famous English batsman E. H. 'Patsy' Hendren, who was in Adelaide coaching, said: 'He was only a teenager then, just a bright, happy, smiling boy with a world to conquer. I could tell, that day in Adelaide, that New South Wales had discovered another champion. Don was a cordial kid who seemed to love batting more than anything in life, even more than fielding along the boundary, in which he took great joy.'

A fortnight later, making his debut for NSW at the Sydney Cricket Ground, he was bowled by the very first ball he faced from Queenslander Frank Gough. He'd pre-empted his shot, rather than playing the delivery on its merits.

His pleasant nature and sheer skill were beginning to win him a host of admirers. He may have been small and slighter than most of his teammates and gripped the bat a little unconventionally, but his wrists were as strong as steel. And even then he had the eye of an eagle. His drives and pull shots were unstoppable and he had the calm temperament and ability to concentrate for long periods like the seasoned players. He still needed to improve his understanding, however, with his fellow batsmen when running between the wickets. But his game improved in these areas, too, assisted by advice from ex-internationals Arthur Mailey and Tommy Andrews who joined him on an end-of-season country tour for the Bohemians. The fixtures including games at Cootamundra and Bowral, Don's home town. Amongst the opposition in another match at Grenfell were four McCabes, including Stan, then just seventeen. The local champion batted at No.3 and made 35 before later opening the bowling. He was a bush prodigy in the Bradman mould and was soon to join the young Don in the NSW and Australian teams.

Grenfell, NSW, prodigy Stan McCabe

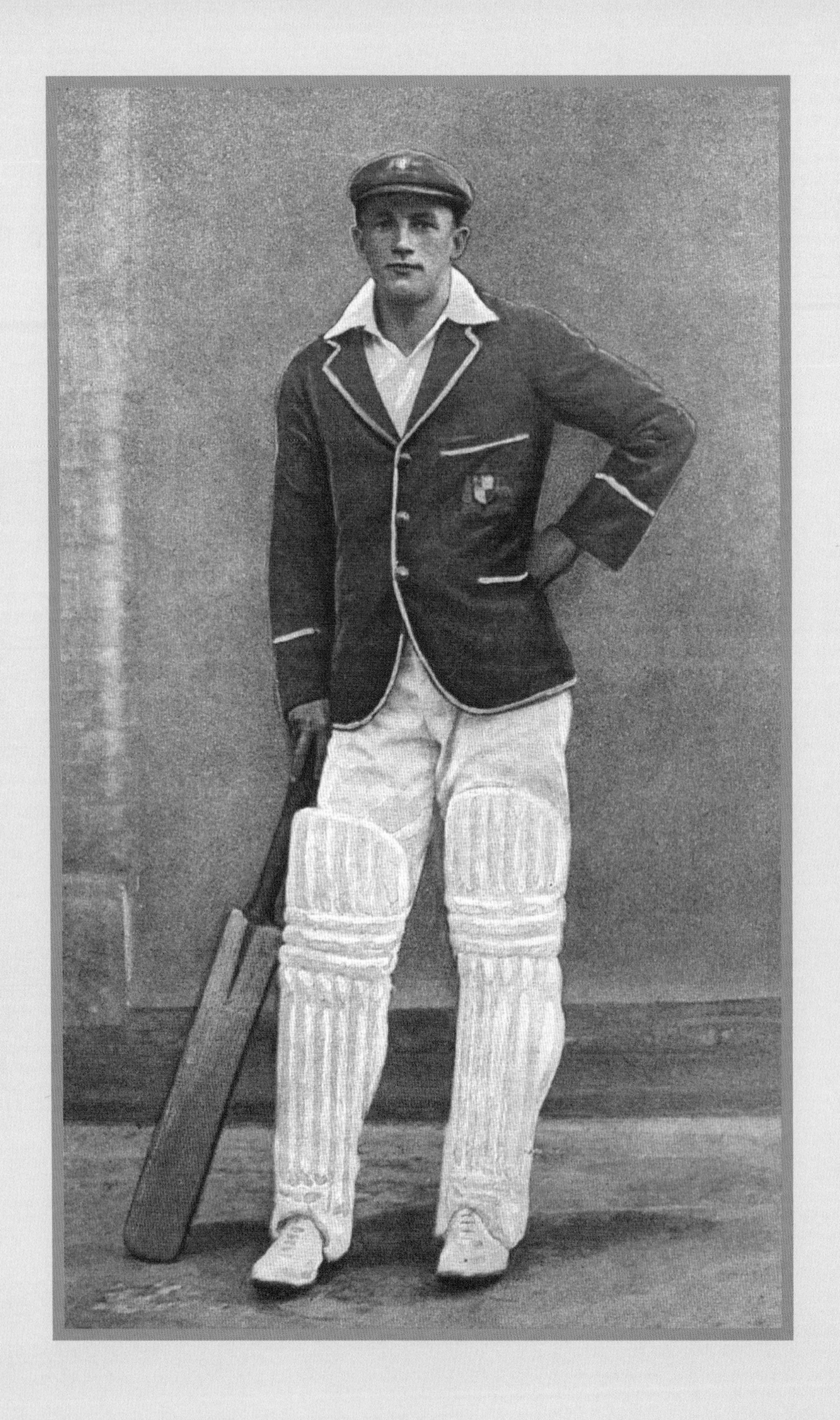

CHAPTER FOUR

'Our Don'

From his first games against England, Don Bradman had a rare flair for the big occasion...

Throughout his first season of representative cricket, Don Bradman lived in Bowral. To make it to Sydney in time for a grade game, he had to make the 5.00 a.m. train and rarely would return before midnight.

In September 1928, he moved to Sydney full-time. The opportunity to practice on St George's turf wickets were a godsend. He looked at the fresh cut grass of the main arena and thought he was in heaven. He thrilled, too, to the prospect of playing against an English team for the first time. England held the Ashes, having won the deciding Test at the Oval in 1926. Among its team were three of the greatest players of them all, Jack Hobbs, Herbert Sutcliffe and Walter Hammond.

Bradman began the season with an uncharacteristic double failure in a Test trial in Melbourne, but played with his normal fluency against the Queenslanders in Brisbane in New South Wales' opening Sheffield Shield game of the summer. Batting at No.3, he made twin centuries, piloting a six-wicket win after the visitors had been set 400-plus to win on a sixth-day wicket. The Queensland attack was strong and included four who had, or were to, represent Australia. He followed, too, with 87 and 132 not out and the light-

OPPOSITE March 1929: the young champion depicted in *The Australian Sporting and Dramatic* newspaper

The Don lived at Rockdale, NSW, for several years after moving full-time to Sydney from the bush in the late 1920s

November, 1926: the Don, seated second from left, scored 37 not out batting No. 7 for the Possibles XV v the Probables XII in his first-ever appearance at the Sydney Cricket Ground. Also pictured, second from the left in the back row, is Australian Rugby Union player-to-be, Syd King

ning run-out of Hammond in the match against Percy Chapman's Englishmen. He had truly announced himself as a Test player in waiting.

'Young Bradman looked as if he could stay forever,' said Hammond. 'None of our bowlers could do any more than feed him runs that day.'

A week later the Australian team for the opening Test was announced and he heard his name read out first on Sydney radio station 2FC. He was the first St George cricketer in history to be selected for Australia. He'd only just turned twenty. The citizens of Bowral (population 2000) were delighted. 'Who would have thought it,' they said. 'Our Don...playing for Australia.'

Terrible Death Dive—Page 3

NEW ADDRESS:
163 PHILLIP STREET
'Phones: BW2071 (8 Lines).

CITY FORECAST:
Warm and Sultry

DAILY TELEGRAPH PICTORIAL

NET SALES EXCEED 141,045 DAILY

No. 15,624 | Registered at the General Post Office, Sydney, for transmission by Post as a newspaper. | SYDNEY: TUESDAY, JANUARY 7, 1930—28 PAGES | Agents' supplies between midnight and 8 a.m., 'PHONE B 1068 or B 1075; after 8, ring BW 2071. | ONE PENNY

DON BRADMAN, BREAKER OF WORLD'S CRICKET RECORDS

HOW DON BRADMAN, CRICKET HE RO, WAS ACCLAIMED by Queenslanders and the Cricket Ground crowd yesterday after his amazing innings of 452, not out. It broke the world's record highest score of 437, made by Ponsford against Queensland in December, 1927. Curiously enough it was in December, 1927 that Bradman, the Bowral youth, played his first Sheffield Shield match. He scored 118 in his initial appearance in first-class cricket, and has since become Australia's most prolific and forceful run-getter. Thirteen centuries is his record in first-class cricket, and there is no saying what new records he will create before 1930 draws to a close.

CHAPTER FIVE

'The boy wonder'

Don Bradman was the youngest Australian to score a Test century – beginning an unparalleled streak of success...

The opening Test of 1928-29 was a first for Don Bradman and Brisbane. Queensland had only just been admitted as a full member of the Sheffield Shield and for the first time it had an Australian Test selector in non-nonsense chairman Jack Hutcheon. The venue for Bradman's debut was the city's Exhibition Ground, the Woolloongabba oval then being under-developed and not considered to be of an appropriate standard to host such an important event. The veteran Victorian Jack Ryder was to be the Don's first Test captain. He was 39. Others in Australia's ageing XI included Charlie Kelleway, 42, Clarrie Grimmett, 36, and 'Gelignite' Jack Gregory, 33. Bradman hadn't even been born when Kelleway played his first Test.

Percy Chapman's MCC team was strong in every area and Bradman's debut match ended in a disastrous 675 run loss, still the biggest in Test history. Chapman was criticised for not asking the Australians to follow-on after his team had led by almost 400 on the first innings. Set 742 to win, the Australians collapsed on the fifth morning for just 66, heavy overnight rains and the uncovered wickets making the pitch a nightmare for batting.

Bradman had never before played on a wet turf pitch and floundered like his teammates, his scores of 18 and 1 seeing him relegated to twelfth-man duties for the second Test in Sydney on the eve of Christmas. His place went to the Queensland allrounder Otto

When Bradman passed Ponsford's mark of 437, the Queenland team gathered around him and gave him three cheers. One by one they shook his hand. Shortly afterwards Kippax closed the innings with Bradman 452 and NSW 8-761, the Queenslanders hoisting Bradman into the air and carrying him off, a picture of which made the front page of Sydney's *Daily Telegraph*. One of the famous ex-players in the pavilion who congratulated Bradman later was Charles Bannerman, scorer of the first century in Test cricket in 1877.

While recovering from a blow to the arm from Harold Larwood in the final Bodyline Test in Sydney, 1933, the Don busied himself with the drinks. He was Australia's official 12th man just once in his long career, after his first Test in 1928-29

BELOW: Otto Nothling, the Queensland all-rounder who replaced the Don after he was dropped

Nothling, who was to make 8 and 44 and go wicketless in 46 eight-ball overs. Never was he to be selected again.

In retrospect, considering the impact Bradman was to have on the game, the boy wonder's dismissal after just one Test must be considered one of the most ill-considered gaffes any selection panel has made. The Australians were again thrashed, this time by eight wickets.

Bradman's return to the team for the New Year Test in Melbourne was virtually automatic, but not condoned by everyone. Ex-Australian captain Warwick Armstrong was one who thought his recall premature: 'For his batting I should have preferred (Gordon) Harris (the South Australian) to Bradman, who will probably be a good player later, but, I think, is not a Test player at present,' he said.

Using an Alan Kippax autographed *Extra Special* bat, Bradman scored 79 in the first innings and 112 in the second. His use of the 'angles' and timing were superb as he used the pace of the bowler to help accelerate the ball through the infield. The crowd went wild with excitement late on the fifth day when the young Don clipped slow bowler J. C. 'Farmer' White through mid-on for an all-run four to give him his century, his first in Tests. For a full five minutes they stood and cheered, waving handkerchiefs and umbrellas and throwing hats in the air. In his tour diary, Hobbs said: 'There was such

November 1928: Australia's X11 for the Don's first Test match. He is sitting between his first two Test captains, Jack Ryder and Bill Woodfull, right. England crushed Australia by 675 runs

January, 1929: stepping off the Sydney Cricket Ground after making his first triple century in representative ranks, against the visiting Victorians. Also pictured is Jack Fingleton

a demonstration that we all sat down on the field while (Ron) Oxenham walked down the pitch and shook Bradman's hand.'

Bradman was the youngest batsman to score a century in Test cricket. News of his 100 created chaos outside the major newspaper offices, where scoreboards had been erected for passers-by. Motor cars hooted, tram bells clanged and passengers cheered and clapped. This century began a runaway wave of success, still unequalled today. It was the first of his 29 Test centuries, including a record nineteen against England. While Australia lost the series, the headlines heralded the arrival of a new batting champion. Since the First World War, only one other, Victoria's Bill Ponsford, had made a Test century under the age of 25.

'The huge crowd (25,391) simply went mad,' said the Don later. 'The English sat down and I rested on my bat until they stopped. But they didn't stop. I have never heard anything like it in my life. I must admit I felt proud. I scarcely become elated over anything but one couldn't help feeling it before that huge crowd.'

He was to score another century, too, in the final Test of the summer in Melbourne, the only match in the rubber won by Australia. In his first Ashes summer, he'd made 468 runs at an average in excess of 65. Harold Larwood had been the leader of England's attack. Ominously, in Sydney, he was accused by Armstrong of bowling deliberately at the batsmen.

Bradman was on a roll, too, with New South Wales, and in-between the third and fourth Test matches, scored 340 not out against Victoria, then a record for the Sydney Cricket Ground. The SCG wicket square consisted of black, hard-as-flint Bulli soil which promoted pace and bounce. It was all but impossible to mark the surface with sprigged boots. Certainly there were no bowlers' footmarks to aim at late in a match. Unlike today, youngsters were taught to deliver and then run off the wicket immediately. Buoyed by Bradman's solo, NSW made a mammoth 6-713 dec., the young maestro batting eight hours and eight minutes and hitting 38 fours. It was his first colossal score at representative level. It was chanceless, too, except for some near run-outs, twice before he'd made his first century and again at 310.

> 'Bradman cornered the strike, allowing even his own captain Alan Kippax just one and two balls an over. Bradman simply bashed the ball everywhere, wherever he wanted to'
>
> *said Hurwood who was to finish with six for 179.*

His new legion of fans marvelled at his consistency and the following season, leading into the 1930 Ashes tour, he continued to play with rare assurance. In 1928-29, he'd amassed 1690 runs at an average of 93. In 1929-30, he made 1586 runs at 113. Ponsford had been dubbed 'The Recordbreaker' after his stunning feats for Victoria in the late '20s, but he was clearly being outstripped by the boy from Bowral. In a Test trial in Sydney, Bradman made 124 and 225. Then, in January, playing against Queensland, again in Sydney, he set a new world record of 452 not out, surpassing Ponsford's record of 437 set two years previously. In the finest innings he said he ever played at the mighty ground, Bradman scored at more than a run a minute and didn't give even one chance.

SCG historian Philip Derriman says the match had been very much alive before Bradman's incredible solo. Alec Hurwood had dismissed him for just three in the first innings and as the Don came out to bat a second time, someone on the Hill yelled to Hurwood: 'You won't get him out again.'

Bradman, 21, had batted for only 415 minutes in this innings and his record was to last for almost 30 years. Of his achievement he said: 'I was not excited. My feeling was one of complete satisfaction.'

Set 770 to win, Queensland was bowled out for 84 in two hours. It was a stunning victory and set the stage for Bradman's first tri-

RACING ALONG

The time factor and the speed with which you score the runs is very important. The 452 which I scored was made in a little over 400 minutes. There are lots and lots and lots of people who have batted longer than that, but they didn't make as many runs because they didn't score at the same pace

The Don

BELOW: the scoreboard tells the story of a chanceless innings

BRADMAN'S 452		
	Mins	Balls
1st 50	51	55
2nd 50	53	67
3rd 50	43	48
4th 50	38	39
5th 50	45	55
6th 50	58	46
7th 50	45	49
8th 50	43	48
9th 50	38	58
452*	415	465

umphant visit to the mother country, in 1930, when he really did become the talk of the cricket world.

Statistician Charles Davis 're-scored' the Don's fabulous '452', his highest ever score in a first-class match and still the highest-ever score in a second innings of a match, surpassing Dr W. G. Grace's 344 in 1876. 'Bradman was fortunate that Sheffield Shield matches were scheduled for four and a half days in 1929-30; the fifth day was abolished after that season,' said Davis, 'as his innings, under later circumstances, would have been curtailed by an earlier declaration.'

He says the Don, 205 not out overnight, may also have appreciated the rest day on Sunday, 5 January. Still, scoring so many in a second innings required extremely fast, sustained scoring and intense concentration. By all accounts, Bradman was rarely troubled by the Queensland bowlers (though 'Pud' Thurlow bowled well and there were near chances on 264 and 345), but the secret of the gigantic score was his discipline, focus and consistency. Bradman was in a rare zone and scored seemingly at will.

The table alongside gives the times and balls faced for the innings milestones.

Judging on the batting times for his 50s, Bradman appeared to be accelerating during his last 100 runs, but he was actually 'farming' the strike while batting with the lower order. Earlier on, when Bradman added 272 with Alan Kippax, and 156 with Stan McCabe, the strike was shared fairly evenly, but he took 70 per cent of the strike in the eighth-wicket stand of 92 off 105 balls with wicketkeeper Hughie Davidson. As Davis says, this is a very difficult percentage to sustain when scoring rapidly, because strike-farming basically means sacrificing scoring opportunities.

The consistency of scoring is emphasised by his session-by-session scoring. Bradman made 85 (in 92 minutes), 120 (101), 105 (106) and 142 (116) runs in each session, all but scoring four centuries in four consecutive sessions. During his monumental knock, he hit 49 fours, 13 threes, 46 twos, 125 singles and no sixes.

Bradman reached his 300 from 310 balls. While extreme, this was not a personal record and was slower than his 369 against Tasmania in 1935-36. The exact number of balls he faced in that innings is unknown, but it was probably similar to the 221 balls faced

THE HISTORIC SCOREBOARD
NSW v Queensland, January 3, 4, 6 & 7, 1930.
NSW First Innings: 235, Queensland First Innings: 227
NSW Second Innings (January 4 & 6 1930)

		Runs	Balls	4s	6s	Mins	Wkt	fow	Ov	Partn	Balls	Mins	Out	Bradman	Bradman BF
A.G. Fairfax	stmp Leeson b Hurwood	10	40	0	0	41	2	33	11.5	11	30	13	Fairfax	7	10
W.C. Andrews	c Levy b Hurwood	16	42	1	0	26	1	22	7.7	22	63	26	Andrews	-	
D.G. Bradman	not out	452	465	49	0	415									
A.F. Kippax (c)	lbw b Rowe	115	144	12	0	145	3	305	50.4	272	313	145	Kippax	162	177
S.J. McCabe	c Leeson b Hurwood	60	95	10	0	81	4	461	73.5	156	186	81	McCabe	254	271
A.E. Marks	c Bensted b Hurwood	5	10	1	0	10	5	469	75.4	8	15	10	Marks	257	276
A.H. Allsopp	b Hurwood	66	105	4	0	93	6	645	101.2	176	209	93	Allsopp	362	378
C.S. Everett	c Goodwin b Hurwood	4	8	0	0	13	7	669	103.8	24	22	13	Everett	382	390
H.L. Davidson	c and b Goodwin	22	32	2	0	48	8	761	117.1	92	105	48	Davidson	452	465
S.J.W. Burt															
H.C. Chilvers															
Extras	(6b, 1lb, 2nb, 2w)	11													
Total	(117.1 overs)	8-761 declared													

Queensland Second Innings: 84
NSW won by 685 runs.

by Charlie Macartney in reaching 300 against Nottingham in 1921, the fastest triple for which 'BF' figures are known. Denis Compton once reached 300 25 minutes faster than Macartney, but he faced 40 more balls.

The 452 has parallels with Brian Lara's 501 off 474 balls in 1994, when Lara, after reaching 300 off 278 balls and 400 off 367, eased off just a little in the latter stages.

CHAPTER SIX

'Bradman's Tour'

It remains the most prolific Test summer of all; the young Don was a cricketing phenomenon...

Don Bradman's life changed irrevocably after his world record 452 not out and fairytale maiden tour of England. Bursting onto the international cricketing stage, his triumphant solo totally overshadowed Australia's Ashes-winning feats and made him a sporting icon for thousands around the world. The still-shy country kid amassed 974 runs at an average of 139.14 in five Tests, including a triple century at Leeds and 254 on his maiden appearance at Lord's, the innings he was to rate as the finest of his life. 'It was an innings in which the ball went exactly to where I wanted it,' he said years later. The Australians scored 6-729 dec., a new record Test score against England.

The 1930s were years of economic hardship throughout the world. But Bradman's phenomenal batting was a unifying, irresistible force for a nation doing it tough with millions out of work and living on the breadline. Teammate Bill Ponsford always claimed Bradman saw the ball two yards quicker than anyone else in the game. Yet when the Don's eyes were tested during the war, his sight wasn't particularly exceptional; in fact it was inferior to many.

So spectacular were the young Don's feats in 1930, during his first trip to England, that Australia re-claimed the Ashes 2-1, hav-

OPPOSITE: wherever he played the adulation for the Don, from admirers of all ages, was quite extraordinary ing been beaten in the opening encounter at Trent Bridge. It was Bradman's first overseas tour and his first ship voyage. The Australian public had great expectations of its 'superman'. But one of England's highest profiled former cricketers, Percy Fender, claimed that Bradman's batting was 'brilliant but unsound', a judgment the young Don was to delight in refuting. From Worcester on, Bradman began a relentless attack on the English bowlers. He scored ten centuries and almost 3000 runs in all, at an average of 98.

In England in 1930 the Don skipped from triumph to triumph

The smiling Don collected a bag full of runs in May, and has started well on June's lot.

March, 1930: a free-flowing net session in Perth preceding the 1930 tour of England

On the first day of the third Test at Leeds, he made 309 not out, with a century in each session. It was a remarkable domination. On the second morning he carried on to 334, a new high in Test cricket. The *Times* headlined its story 'BRADMAN V ENGLAND' and said his knock was 'incomparable'.

The prospect of seeing the young colonial record-breaker

Bill Woodfull was the Don's captain during the 1930 and 1934 tours of England

RESPONSIBILITY FREE

'In the 1930 matches I did not feel the constraint of responsibility which by force of circumstances so dominated my career from 1936 until its close'

Don Bradman

'It was Bradman, Bradman all the way. It is almost impossible to describe his innings, because it was all of a piece. Any one period of it was just like any other'

A man in the crowd

BRADMAN'S FIGURES TEST BY TEST, FOR 1930

First Test (Nottingham) 8 & 131
Second Test (Lord's) 254 & 1
Third Test (Leeds) 334
Fourth Test (Manchester) 14
Fifth Test (The Oval) 232

ensured packed pavilions and grandstands around the country and triggered record financial gains. In a message of congratulations to the Australians, King George V singled Bradman out for individual praise. 'He is a cricketing phenomenon,' said English cricket stalwart P. F. 'Plum' Warner.

Bradman played relentless, risk-free cricket, rarely lifting the ball. In particular he scored heavily from drives, on both sides of the wicket. Though it was achieved more than 50 years ago, on uncovered wickets, this record is still quoted in amazement by cricketing enthusiasts.

While he was away, Bradman received thousands of fan letters and telegrams. His mother, Emily, at home in Bowral said: 'If these records continue much longer, I don't know how I am going to stand it. I'm so worked up and so excited when Don is playing in the great matches that I don't know what I'm doing. Although I'm so proud of him — and what mother would not be, I am not the least bit afraid of his success turning his head as it might do with most young fellows. I know my Don would think too much about his mother to let success spoil him.'

Bradman's phenomenal solos had an effect on the whole game of cricket. No opposing team ever felt safe from defeat. Even if it made a good score it was always possible that Bradman alone might match it. The summer of 1930 is still called 'Bradman's tour'. On departure from St Pancras station, he told one interviewer: 'It isn't goodbye, it is only *au revoir*. I hope to be back in 1934 if my cricket is still good enough.'

'Bradman literally jumped at the chance to show his mastery, and (Jack) White was known afterwards to say that such was Don's speed of eye and foot he believed he need never have let him bounce unless he had wanted to. But Bradman was at home with everyone'

E. W. 'Jim' Swanton

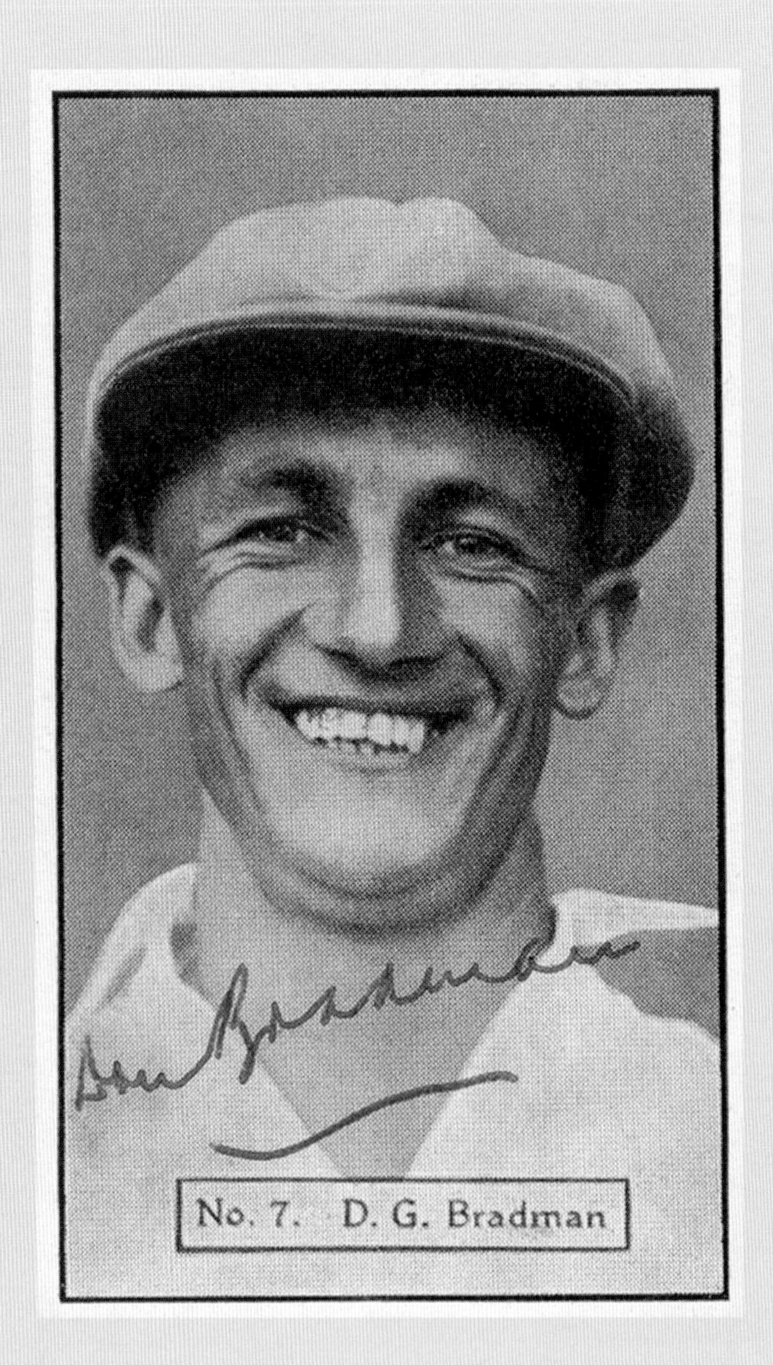
No. 7. D. G. Bradman

CHAPTER SEVEN

The darling of Australia

Don Bradman 's spectacular feats made him a hero as Australia was plunged into the toughest possible economic times...

No-one was more important to the Australian psyche than Don Bradman in the early 1930s. Times were tough after the fall of Wall St, the economic backlash was considerable and unemployment rife as families battled to survive.

The West Indies toured Australia for the first time in 1930-31 and South Africa in 1931-32. They were triumphant summers for Bradman in which he continued to reel off century after century, including 152 in the fourth Test against the Windies in his 100th innings in first-class cricket. To that time, however, his batting statistics in first-class cricket were only a little superior to the Victorian batting colossus Bill Ponsford:

	Inns	NO	Runs	HS	Ave	100s
The Don	100	15	7948	452*	93.50	29
Ponsford	100	7	7196	437	77.37	28

* denotes not out

A youthful-looking Don in the nets wearing his blue NSW cap

Bradman's highest Test score in Australia of 299 not out was achieved the next season in the fourth international against the South Africans in Adelaide.

In Brisbane in the opening Test of the summer, he'd made 226, after being dropped twice, at 11 and 15 from the bowling of Neville Quinn. In Melbourne, Bradman's century in 98 minutes was the fastest of his career. One pull shot against the bowling of Cyril Vincent flew to the boundary like a rifle shot. He seemed keen to score his 100 before stumps but lost the strike in the last over and was 92 not out at the close.

In all, the Don made centuries in six consecutive matches against the Springboks and averaged a gargantuan 201 in the Tests. His driving was powerful and precise and back-foot play spectacular. Few in Australian cricket, even the old masters, had ever used the whole crease like the twinkle-toed Don.

As news of his dominance spread, the crowds doubled and tripled. Shops and businesses closed early. It seemed everyone had appointments in and around whichever ground Don was at. Postal authorities across the eastern seaboard reported that the normal volumes of mail were down, a direct result of businessmen being away from their desks when the cricket was in town.

One newspaper labelled the Don as 'cricket's Walter Lindrum', after Australia's world champion billiards player renowned for his record breaks. By then, the Don had made more than 9000 runs in just five seasons and taken run-making to a new level.

In April 1932, aged 23, he married Jessie Menzies, his childhood sweetheart from Bowral days. It was to be a long and extremely happy marriage. 'Jessie has been the best partner of my life,' he'd often say. The honeymooners went to America and Canada in 1932 with Arthur Mailey's private team. Fifty-two games were scheduled in which the Don, the principal drawcard, made 3782 runs at an average of 100.21, including fifteen centuries in Canada and three in the United States. His highest score was 260, the record score ever made in Canada, on a matting pitch over turf at the Ontario Reformatory in Guelph. At New York's Yankee Stadium, he met America's baseball star Babe Ruth and in Hollywood fielded in the slips to Boris Karloff of horror movies fame. He also met and was photographed with some of the most glamorous screen actors and actresses of the time, including Jean Harlow, Clark Gable, Mary Astor and Myrna Loy.

Victor Richardson, Stan McCabe, Alan Kippax, Hanson Carter and a young 'Chuck' Fleetwood-Smith were among the happy tourists. It was to be a pleasurable lull leading into cricket's stormiest season, the acrimonious bodyline summer of 1932-33.

Jessie Menzies, who the Don said was 'the best partner' of his life

> 'When second slip dropped Bradman early in his innings [South Africa's] Bruce Mitchell was heard to emit an expletive which few of his friends believed part of his vocabulary. This short four-letter word had scarcely escaped from him before he dropped Bradman himself'
>
> *R. S. 'Dick' Whitington*

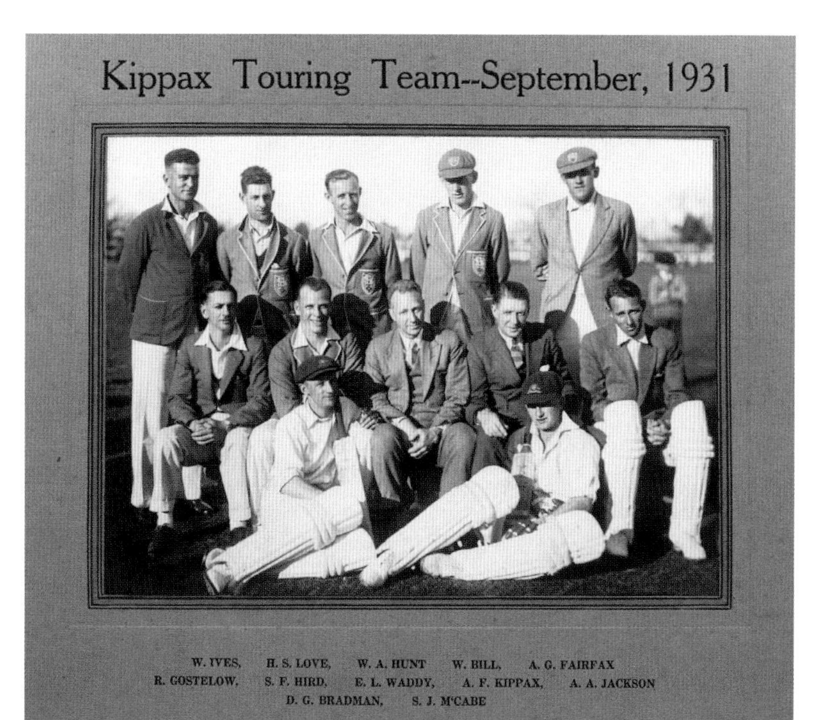

'In retrospect,' said the Don of his tour experience, 'I would not have missed the trip for anything and many a happy hour has been spent over the last 60-odd years talking about the beauty of the Canadian Rockies and other pleasant recollections of a unique trip.'

MIDDLE RIGHT: a honeymooning Don met baseball giant Babe Ruth at Yankee Stadium, 1932

BOTTOM RIGHT: cricket's Walter Lindrum with the billiards master himself

LEFT, June 1932: in Vancouver. Back row, left to right, Edgar Rofe, Bill Ives, Keith Tolhurst, 'Chuck' Fleetwood-Smith, 'Dick' Nutt, Phil Carney. Front row, Stan McCabe, the Don, Arthur Mailey (manager), Vic Richardson (captain), Alan Kippax, Hanson Carter

CHAPTER EIGHT

Evil, insidious, brutal bodyline

It wasn't cricket and almost caused a temporary cessation of Anglo-Australian relations...

The English team which toured Australia in 1932-33 gained an unwanted notoriety during cricket's wildest summer of all. In totally flaunting the spirit of cricket, the MCC's iron-willed captain Douglas Jardine endangered imperial relations and triggered the game's biggest controversy.

Jardine decided that the only way to stop Don Bradman's streak of big scores was to bowl directly at him and make him fear for his own safety. If he defended, he risked being caught in the leg trap; if he hooked, there was the prospect of top-edging the ball to the two deep fieldsmen on the leg side.

Jardine succeeded above and beyond his wildest dreams and regained the Ashes 4-1, but history records him with chequered affection, some labelling him as a fanatic and even a coward for his obsessive win-at-all-costs philosophy.

His fast bowlers, Nottinghamshire pair Harold Larwood and Bill Voce, pitched their high-speed deliveries directly at the batsman rather than at the wicket.

The English team hoped that the bodyline tactics would upset Bradman destroy his concentration. Jardine, leading on tour for the first time, was an aloof figure on the steamer the *Orantes*, keeping his own company and fine-tuning his tactics, which at that point

His skull fractured, Bert Oldfield reels from the wicket in Adelaide

OPPOSITE: Australia's Fourth Test team, Brisbane, February, 1933.
Back row, left to right, Bert Tobin (12th man), Tim Wall, Bill O'Reilly, 'Bert' Ironmonger, Ernie Bromley. Seated, Hammy Love, Bill Ponsford, Vic Richardson, Bill Woodfull, Stan McCabe, Don Bradman, Len Darling

RIGHT: Harold Larwood decimated Australia, then never played Test cricket again

BELOW: Another Adelaide victim, this time it's captain Bill Woodfull

> 'Bodyline is dangerous. I believe that only good luck is responsible for the fact that no-one was killed by bodyline'
>
> *England's champion batsman Walter Hammond*

were still highly secretive. He didn't float his plans even with his manager, P. F. 'Plum' Warner, a former captain and one of the selectors who had chosen him to bring the Ashes back home.

Jardine felt Bradman's mountainous scores were unlikely to be restricted by conventional means, especially on the flat Australian wickets after the new ball lost its shine. Bradman had thrashed England's bowling in 1930 and had made centuries in each of the four Tests in which he batted in the previous Australian season against the South Africans. He was at the top of his game. If England wanted to regain the Ashes, Bradman had to be stopped, no matter the cost. Jardine believed Bradman to be vulnerable against the shorter ball delivered at high pace. Later, when he made the tactics public, he reminded Warner of the incident at The Oval in 1930 when

Bradman, on 175, was struck under the heart by Larwood on a soft wicket and for a time his footwork hadn't been quite as assured. In Australia, he intended to pepper the Don and all the other top-line Australians with as much short-pitched bowling as possible. For Jardine, winning was everything.

Warner was fiercely opposed and pleaded with Jardine to think of the good of the game. The two argued heatedly and Jardine, unhappy at his authority being questioned, excluded Warner from almost every meaningful conversation for the remainder of the tour.

Twenty-eight-year-old Nottinghamshire coalminer Larwood was to be Australia's chief tormentor. He had gained fresh levels of fitness and a yard or two of extra pace. He may have been smaller than most express bowlers, but he was faster than ever and very accurate. His bouncer tended to skid through at shoulder height and he had everyone ducking, Bradman included. Helped by Jardine's leg-side fields, Larwood, Voce and, in one Test, Bill Bowes effectively hosed down the Bradman menace.

With the series square at 1-1, the Third Test in Adelaide saw Australia's popular wicketkeeper Bert Oldfield suffer a skull fracture, while attempting to hook a Larwood bouncer. Australia's steadfast captain Bill Woodfull was twice struck tremendous blows in the chest by Larwood. Years later his wife said she believed the hits had shortened his life.

There was a near riot when Oldfield was felled. The angry crowd hooted the Englishmen and counted Larwood out. Vic Richardson believed if one person had jumped the fence, hundreds more would have followed, endangering the safety of the English, especially Jardine and Larwood. Bill O'Reilly said there would have almost certainly been a riot had the game been in Melbourne or Sydney and not the city of churches, Adelaide.

Defying his captain's orders to stay in behind the flight of the ball, Bradman had devised his own plan to counter the bodyline attack and make himself a moving target. Sometimes he'd draw away to the leg side of the wicket, sometimes to the off. With determination, skill and judgment he did not miss any opportunity to slash the ball through the virtually vacant off side. His tactics worked but didn't impress everyone, including his captain, Woodfull. He scored at a rapid rate, however, believing that runs, not bruises, were paramount. He often employed very unorthodox cross-bat strokes, but he was determined to land some punches before he was 'pinged' himself.

'We call it bodyline bowling but it is really bowling at the man. If the members of the MCC (Marylebone Cricket Club) had seen this attack in operation in Australia there would be no doubt about their attitude'

Former Australian captain, Clem Hill

England's bodyline protagonists: from top left, captain Douglas Jardine and fast bowlers Harold Larwood, Bill Bowes and Bill Voce

NOWHERE TO RUN

We were upset with what they did. There was absolutely nowhere to go. If I had stood exactly where I was the ball would have hit me in the chest or higher

The Don

Leo O'Brien witnessed Bill Woodfull's famous rebuke to England's manager 'Plum' Warner

In eight matches, Bradman was struck by Larwood only once, but his batting average was slashed to a modest 56 in the Tests (he played four of the five matches, missing the first with illness) and England careered to a commanding series victory. Bradman's only century came in the second innings in Melbourne, when he accelerated to 103 not out, being helped to his century by St Kilda veteran Bert Ironmonger, then 50 years of age.

Jardine cared neither about the Australian public's resentment of fast leg theory, nor the possibility of reprisals. He bristled, though, when Woodfull dared question the tactics in Adelaide, after manager Warner had visited him to check on the severity of his Larwood-inflicted bruises. 'I do not wish to see you, Mr Warner,' said Woodfull. 'There are two sides out there. One is trying to play cricket and the other is not.'

Leo O'Brien was Australia's twelfth man in that game and was one of the few in the room within earshot. Years later he still remembered Warner's flushed face as he hurried from the rooms.

Since the opening weeks of the tour when Larwood and his burly ally Voce bowled directly at every Australian state team, there had been a tidal wave of protest. By mid-summer Richardson was taking block 45 cm outside his leg stump and the ball was still coming directly at him. The Australian batsmen expected to be hit. There were 34 instances in the Tests; Larwood was responsible for 25.

On the slower English wickets, the 1930 Australians had mainly been untroubled, but on the harder, faster wickets of Australia, even the most agile and quick-footed players like Bradman were hit. Larwood bowled at around 145 km/h, faster than almost anyone before him.

Woodfull was struck seven times in four Tests and his opening partner Ponsford, six in three. Ponny would turn his back on the ball and allow it to strike him, rather than running the risk of popping up a catch to the close-in English fieldsmen. Ponsford said cricket lost a lot of meaning for him during that summer. He was to play only one more home Test and retired at the conclusion of the '34 Ashes series, aged 33, despite having just made his highest Test score, 266.

By the tour's end even the English fielders had stopped trying to sympathise with the retreating Australian batsmen. There was no camaraderie between the sides, Jardine being made to wait in the corridor whenever he wanted to see Woodfull. The Australians referred to Jardine as 'the bastard' and many wanted to retaliate.

LEFT, February, 1933: the Don is bowled by Harold Larwood in the final Test in Sydney.

ABOVE: former bodyline adversary Bill Bowes greets the Don at London's Tilbury docks in 1948

Test umpire George Hele said Jardine had flaunted cricket's good name and any repetitions would have been incredibly harmful to the game's popularity.

Larwood was to take 33 wickets for the series before fracturing a bone in his left foot in the final Test in Sydney. When Bradman was dismissed for 71, Larwood, limping from the exertions of his ferocious bowling, quietly followed him to the Sydney pavilion. His job was completed. He was never to play a Test again and was virtually exiled from the game on his return to England.

In time, the laws of the game were to be altered to stop bodyline by allowing only two players behind square leg.

Bradman's brilliance went undimmed at club level and in five appearances with St George in 1932-33 he scored 108 not out, 105 not out, 112, 134 and 53. He also scored more than 1000 runs in first-class cricket for the fifth consecutive summer.

He (Bill Bowes) bowled it exactly where I expected he would and I played the shot chest high as I intended to play it, but by a miracle I pulled it down to the base of my leg-stump. I could try it 1000 times again and I couldn't do it again.

Don Bradman

The determination to win at any price was deplorable.

Dr Reg Bettington, a former NSW player and ex-captain of Oxford University

"Jardine planned for us, he cared for us, he fought for us on that tour and he was so faithful in everything he did that we were prepared on our part to do anything we could for him"

England opener, Herbert Sutcliffe

Get ready to duck: Jardine's controversial bodyline field

I doubt if England could have won the rubber without bodyline bowling. If it had not been used, Bradman, for one, would have made buckets of runs. He is a better batsman than ever ... If this sort of attack is persisted in, somebody will be killed sooner or later. If I had to play this type of bowling, I would get out of cricket ... The Australian batsmen had my sympathy.

legendary Englishman Jack Hobbs

If Jardine's team won the Ashes fairly and squarely by certain methods in Australia (and the MCC maintained that the methods were fair and square) why were we not allowed to try and keep the Ashes by similar methods in this country (in 1934)?

Arthur Carr, former England and Nottinghamshire captain, sacked in 1934

It may be our last Test if the squealing goes on ... It is about time that the Test cricket farce was ended. Throughout the world the Australians are branded as squealers and bad sportsmen.

Queensland fast bowler Hugh 'Pud' Thurlow

'We have seen sufficient of bodyline bowling this season to realise that it does more to kill cricket than any other force ever brought into play... it's premeditated brutality...with a speed merchant like Larwood, the element of physical danger is so great that in the interests of cricket he should not use it'

ex-Australian captain M. A. 'Monty' Noble

There were occasions when any normal captain would have been ruffled by the unprecedented incidents, due solely to England's bowling methods, but to the credit of Woodfull it must be said that no captain could have led his side in a more restrained and exemplary manner.

Australian wicketkeeper Bert Oldfield

Jardine bore much harsh treatment and barracking in Australia with dignity and courage. He considered that this type of bowling was within the law, but I fancy that he would admit that it was a stern policy.

P. F. 'Plum' Warner, ex-English captain and manager of the 1932-33 team

BODYLINE REVISITED

There were casualties galore from bodyline, on both sides, but surprisingly it took years before administrators limited the number of fieldsmen allowed behind square leg.

Arthur Morris recalled that in Sydney one day during the 1946-47 season he encountered an over of bodyline from Victoria's Keith Miller and promptly hooked five fours in an over!

'It was a greentop, Keith Carmody got a one and I was on strike,' said Morris. 'Lindsay (Hassett) had six behind square leg. It was a sea of black caps out there. I was amazed they didn't all bump into each other. Douglas Jardine would have been jealous of that field,' he said.

'You didn't need to be a Phillip St lawyer to know what was to come. Keith bounced me and kept on bouncing me and I kept on hooking him. One bouncer wasn't at the body but short on the off side. Having played a lot of tennis I smashed it for three through the covers.

'Miller was very quick but by the end of the over he was spitting chips!' (His fourteen overs that day were to cost 79 runs for just one wicket.)

'Lindsay couldn't have got away with it for long. It was straight out bodyline stuff.'

BRADMAN v BODYLINE

	Balls received	Runs scored
Off Larwood	151	115
Off Voce	64	42
Off Bowes	7	9
Off Allen	131	109
Off Hammond	93	71
Off Verity	73	44
Off Mitchell	10	6
Totals	529	396

Scoring rate: 74.85 runs per 100 balls

CHAPTER NINE

A mere mortal

There was a dramatic finish to Don Bradman's 1934 tour when he developed acute appendicitis...

The bodyline furore saw the MCC act emphatically and by the time the 1934 Australians arrived in England, Harold Larwood was no longer in England's XI. Douglas Jardine, too, had been ostracised. Don Bradman was Australia's new vice-captain and while he'd had some health problems, he started the campaign as he had in 1930, with a double century at Worcester.

In the first three Tests, however, he made only 29, 25, 36, 13 and 30. He complained of back strain, muscular injuries and allergies, abdominal pains, even a throat infection and went thirteen innings without scoring a century. Critics claimed him to have been too reckless, particularly in the Tests. However, playing with his old measured poise, he scored 304, his second Test triple century at Leeds and finished with 244 and 77 in the fifth Test, at The Oval.

Even one of the original bodyliners, Yorkshireman Bill Bowes, could not restrict Bradman. Although the Australians were robbed of victory when rain stopped play in the fourth Test, they won the decider. The English attack had been strong and competitive, but the team's fielding fell away especially late in the tour.

So sore was Bradman after his Headingley triumph that team-mates had to undress him and carry him to the massage table. He

D. G. BRADMAN

OPPOSITE, August, 1934: the Don plays Bill Bowes through the leg-side on his way to 244 at The Oval

July 1934: with Bill Ponsford during their epic stand of 388 at Leeds after Australia had fallen to 3-39. The Don made 304 and 'Ponny' 181

SIX FAMOUS TRANSFERS

Don Bradman - NSW to South Australia

Greg Chappell - South Australia to QLD

Adam Gilchrist - NSW to Western Australia

Neil Harvey - Victoria to NSW

Stuart MacGill - Western Australia to NSW

Keith Miller - Victoria to NSW

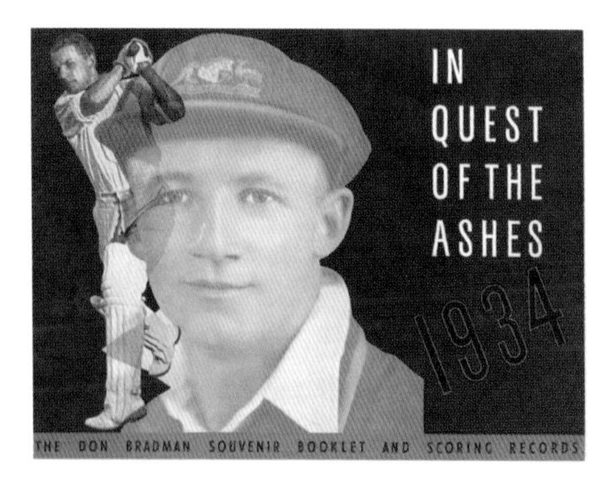

injured a thigh muscle, too, while fielding later in the game and was an enforced onlooker for all six matches in between the fourth and final Tests. Throughout his Leeds triple, he carried a telegram from wife Jessie in his pocket. It read: 'Go to it, Don. I believe in you.'

Less than a month after the final Test, a fatigued Bradman was found to have acute appendicitis. The effects of the long English tour had caught up with him. He was seriously ill and rumours spread that he had actually died on the operating table. His fans prayed for him. Offers of blood transfusions from worried fans flooded the hospital. The P & O shipping company offered Jessie a free trip to England on the *Maloja* and after a 31-day passage, she joined her husband. His convalescence took some time and the couple stayed in Scotland for nearly two months while he recuperated.

Down-time for Don and the Australians during the 1934 tour. They were to regain the Ashes in the deciding Test at The Oval

On his departure for Australia, the Don happened to be on the same railway platform as Winston Churchill, the future Prime Minister of England. The two famous men met and were photographed together for the newspapers. Although he returned home to a hero's welcome, Bradman, on doctor's orders, was unable to participate in the 1934-35 Sheffield Shield season and was unavailable, too, for the 1935 Australian tour of South Africa. However, Bradman still had an ambition to be realised: he wanted to captain his country.

CHAPTER TEN

Captain of Australia

Having missed eighteen months of cricket, Don Bradman's goal was to return for the Ashes summer of 1936-37...

He may have been the outstanding cricketer in the world, but the Depression years had been tough and Don Bradman, despite his celebrity status and involvement in a range of endorsements, was still not as financially secure as he desired. Cricket was only a leisure and paid accordingly. All the players had jobs and Bradman was keen to find a job outside the game which could guarantee long-term security for Jessie and him. When the opportunity arose to move into a new business, in stockbroking in Adelaide, he took it. Several wealthy stockbrokers had paid their way to be a part of Arthur Mailey's private tour in 1932 and had encouraged the young Don to think about life after cricket. His new employer, Harry Hodgetts, was on the South Australian Cricket Association executive and a delegate to the Board of Control. The Hodgetts offer of £600 a year was irresistible. He was also given a new Chevrolet Roadstar as well as the promise of all the time off he needed to practise and play cricket. When his move had been mooted, a friend contacted the NSW Cricket Association only to be told that special assistance for Bradman would be setting a dangerous precedent! The Bradmans initially moved in with Hodgetts in up-market Kensington Park to allow the Don to qualify for South Australia for the 1934-35 season.

His illness precluded him, however, from playing for his new

OPPOSITE, December 1936: the Don tossing the coin for the first time as Australia's captain, with England's 'Gubby' Allen, in Brisbane. Allen called correctly and Australia was bowled out twice in under 100 overs and lost the Test by an innings

state until the following summer, in 1935-36, and the results were spectacular. In five matches he scored almost 800 runs at an average of 123. Included was a mammoth 357 against Victoria in Melbourne, proof that a little of his old hunger and focus had returned. The Don was still cricket's batting powerhouse. Stan Quin was keeping wickets for Victoria and said when Bradman was on strike, he couldn't remember taking even one ball. There was widespread joy, too, throughout the cricket-loving public when the Don made a double century in the opening match of the 1936-37 season in a virtual Test trial against Vic Richardson's Australian tourists, who had been in South Africa. He was immediately named Test captain.

His fortunes were to truly shape the series like no other he was to be involved in. In Brisbane, where Australia was caught on a wet wicket, he made 38 and 0 and the Australians were thrashed. In Sydney, in another rain-affected match, he made 0 and 82 and the Australians lost by an innings. With the Australians 2-0 down, Bradman's captaincy was questioned, some favouring the return of the veteran Richardson, who had been so successful in South Africa.

The Ashes were on the line as the third Test opened in Melbourne on New Year's Day. The match was to go into a sixth day and attracted more than 350,000 fans, the ground's biggest ever match attendance — superior even to the Centenary Test 40 years on. So huge were the crowds, especially on the Monday when a new world record of 87,798 gathered, that many scrambled over barriers and into the last uncompleted bays of the club's new Southern Stand.

Author Keith Dunstan said Melbourne came to a standstill like never before during Test week. Important decisions like raising the cost of a loaf of bread were put on hold as all of cricket-mad Melbourne was engrossed in the great match, either going to the ground or listening on their radiograms. Bradman could make only 13 as Australia reached 6-181 on the rain-interrupted opening day. Stan McCabe (63) fell immediately on the second, play not starting until 2.15 p.m. and on a difficult wicket which the sun was rapidly drying, Bradman declared at nine down, not even bothering to give his No.11, L. O'B. 'Chuck' Fleetwood-Smith, a hit.

For the first time in many years, England had neither of its Melbourne specialists, Hobbs nor Sutcliffe, to repel the Australians and they tumbled to 9-76 before England's captain G.O. 'Gubby' Allen, too, declared, the wicket still full of venom. Allen had opted not to declare earlier as rain was threatening. As it was, there was time only for two overs because of bad light and more showers. Bradman recast his order, sending in O'Reilly and Fleetwood-Smith. While O'Reilly fell first ball, ballooning a return catch back to Voce, Bradman sent in another tailender, Frank Ward. At 1-3, the game was still deliciously poised.

Sunday was gloriously fine and Monday's play produced a record crowd of 87,798. Against the odds Ward batted an hour and Keith Rigg for two. By mid-afternoon the pitch had settled and Jack Fingleton, batting at No.6 and Bradman, in at No.7, had mastered the bowling, adding 97 for the sixth wicket. Rain interrupted play on three occasions, making it difficult for spinners Hedley Verity and Walter Robins to adequately grip the ball. With Bradman 56 not out overnight, there were almost 65,000 in attendance on the Tuesday, all willing their hero to his first century as Australia's captain.

The new ball was taken early on the third day and just 56 runs added but without a wicket. It was the crucial session of the match and once Bradman snicked a four from Voce shortly after the interval to bring up his ton — his sixth at the ground in seven Tests, breaking Hobbs' mark of five 100s in ten — he and Fingleton started to play with freedom and authority. They weren't to be separated until late in the final session, having added a monumental 346 to make the Test match safe and create a set of new records, several of which are still in place. The most notable are:

- the highest sixth-wicket partnership in any first-class match in Australia (surpassing 323 by E. H. 'Patsy' Hendren and Johnny Douglas for MCC against Victoria in 1920-21);
- and the highest partnership (at the time) for any wicket for any Test in Australia, (surpassing the 323 by openers Hobbs and Wilfred Rhodes for England against Australia, also in Melbourne in 1911-12).

Bradman batted the entire day and was 248 not out at stumps and Australia safe at 6-500. The Don had made 192 runs for the day, another record, surpassing Clem Hill's 182 on the opening day of the Melbourne Test in 1897-98.

'He more or less beat us off his own bat,' said Englishman Hammond. Bradman scored 270 and Fingleton 136. Australia

BELOW, December, 1936: the Don had two visits to the wicket on the last Saturday before Christmas in Sydney. The Australians were caught on a sticky wicket, dismissed for just 80 and forced to follow-on. After a first-ball duck in the first innings, the Don drives England's Hedley Verity on his way to 82 in the second

reached 564 and bowled England out a second time for 323 to win convincingly, O'Reilly and Fleetwood-Smith sharing eight wickets between them.

Bill Brown, who batted at No.5 in the Australian second innings, said the whole see-sawing match was an unforgettable experience. 'It was an amazing feeling just to be involved,' he said. 'Every time you caught a ball there'd be tremendous applause from the huge crowd. And that was only at fielding practice!' It had been a massive turnaround and the Australians carried their new momentum into Adelaide where they again won easily. The series was tied 2-2, with the decisive match back in Melbourne.

Paceman Kenneth Farnes had returned for the Adelaide Test, taking five wickets in a game also notable for yet another double century from Bradman. In the final three Tests the Don had batted for more than nineteen hours, his focus and concentration as intense as at any time in his career. He'd also showed himself to be a great leader, planning his tactics in advance and taking time and care to study the form of his own and the opposing players. He organised his field placings with the precision of a general before a battle. As captain of Australia, too, he made many fine after-dinner speeches and was a wonderful ambassador.

> He (Bradman) had gained valuable experience as a Test captain and had shown himself to have an active and perceptive cricket brain, not least in the third Test at Melbourne when he had outmanoeuvred Allen
>
> *Charles Williams*

ABOVE LEFT, December 1936: Australia's Second Test team in Sydney.
Back row, left to right, Jackie Badcock (inset), Arthur Chipperfield, Ernie McCormick, Morrie Sievers, Bill O'Reilly, Frank Ward.
Seated, Ray Robinson (12th man), Leo O'Brien, Stan McCabe, the Don, Jack Fingleton, Bert Oldfield

CHAPTER ELEVEN

1000 runs before the end of May

Don Bradman's phenomenal runscoring feats went unchallenged before the dark years of the World War II...

In 1938, Australia and England drew the Test series, just four Tests being played instead of five, the third scheduled Test at Old Trafford being abandoned without a toss being made, or a ball bowled.

Bradman's scoring was phenomenal, though his strokeplay was a little more measured than in his non-captaincy days. He became the first batsman in history to average more than 100 runs an innings in an English season and for the second time he amassed 1000 runs before the end of May. No other batsman has ever emulated this achievement. His century to start the series at Trent Bridge was important as Australia forced a draw after England had started with almost 700, batting first. The Don was unable to bat in the final match at The Oval, having broken his ankle while bowling. In this match, Englishman Len Hutton made a record-breaking Test score of 364, a feat which surpassed Bradman's 334 at Leeds in 1930. In this final match Australia was beaten by an innings, but the Ashes were still Australia's and were to remain so for another fifteen years.

By now there was a threat of war in Europe, but cricket continued, the government keen for as much sport to be played as per normal. Bradman made six centuries in a row in the second-last Aus-

OPPOSITE, January, 1940: one of the Don's last innings at his favourite Sydney Cricket Ground was against New South Wales. Umpire George Borwick emphatically adjudged him lbw to Bill 'Tiger' O'Reilly for 39. Also pictured are Ron Saggers (wicketkeeper), 'Ginty' Lush, 'Dick' Whitington (the non-striker) and Arthur Chipperfield

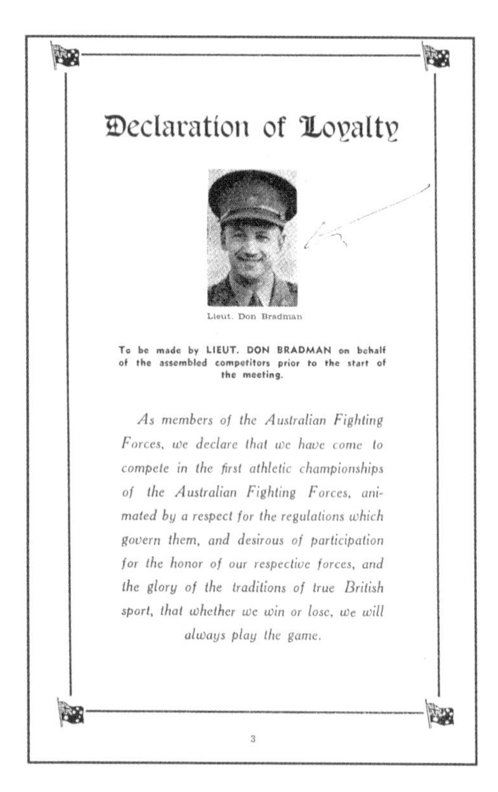

Declaration of Loyalty

Lieut. Don Bradman

To be made by LIEUT. DON BRADMAN on behalf of the assembled competitors prior to the start of the meeting.

As members of the Australian Fighting Forces, we declare that we have come to compete in the first athletic championships of the Australian Fighting Forces, animated by a respect for the regulations which govern them, and desirous of participation for the honor of our respective forces, and the glory of the traditions of true British sport, that whether we win or lose, we will always play the game.

3

TOP: with much-loved Scottish professional golfer Sandy Herd during the 1938 tour

TOP RIGHT, August, 1938: the Don is helped from The Oval after breaking a bone in his ankle during England's record 903 for 7 declared

tralian season before the Second World War, equalling C. B. Fry's world record. In the 1939-40 season, at the age of 32, the Don was batting as well as ever and again made more than 1000 runs.

The war, however, stopped the planned 1940-41 English tour down under and when Japan entered the war, all cricket was abandoned. Bradman joined the army as a lieutenant, but was dogged by ill-health. In November 1940, he returned to the MCG for the first Australian Fighting Forces Athletic Track Championships and after the opening ceremony by Prime Minister Bob Menzies, the Don made the declaration of loyalty on behalf of the assembled servicemen. Getting into the spirit of the events he also raced 'Chuck' Fleetwood-Smith in a fun event, with Menzies the line judge. One of my uncles, Bob Piesse, ran for the Navy that day and said, despite a small crowd, the aura surrounding Bradman was unforgettable.

DON BRADMAN'S 1000 RUNS

BEFORE THE END OF MAY

258	v Worcestershire
58	Oxford University
137	Cambridge University
278	MCC
2	Northamptonshire
143	Surrey
145 not out	Hampshire
5 & 30 not out	Middlesex

1056 runs at 150.85 (from 30 April 1938 to 31 May 1938)

'It was an innings (at Trent Bridge) absolutely different from anything we had seen from him before... this time his nose was on the pitch and his enemy was the clock. The wicket itself had worn. It was dusty and the spinners could turn. It called for all the concentration in the world'

A. G. 'Johnnie' Moyes

'Every eye was on him; the events themselves were almost immaterial,' he said.

A recurrence of fibrositis was to lead to the Don's premature discharge from the army on medical grounds. He'd complained of a 'frozen' shoulder, as well as paralysis in his hand. His eyesight had also been causing him problems and he was unable to play cricket at all for two years. As the war escalated, some doubted that he would play again.

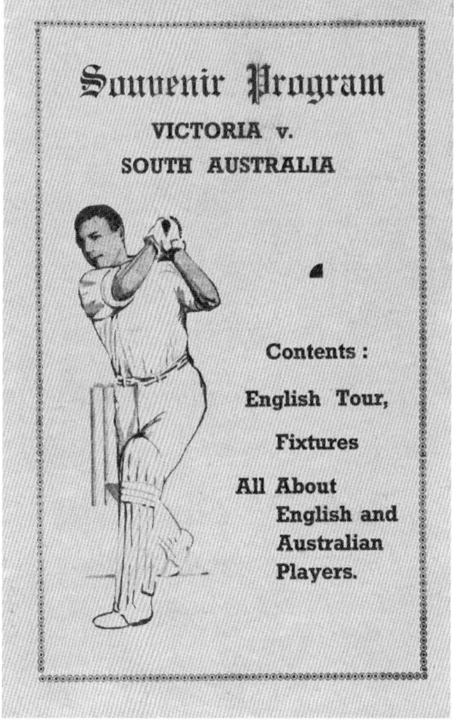

CHAPTER TWELVE

Doing it for his son

Central in Don Bradman's return to cricket after years of illness was a promise he made to his wife Jessie...

If there was one conversation important in Don Bradman's resuming cricket after the war it was the one he had with wife Jessie, who simply said how it would be nice if young John, Bradman's son, could get to see him play. Bradman had been ill for some time and while he helped select the team to New Zealand in 1945-46, he was not well enough to lead it, in what turned out to be the first Test between the Australasian neighbours. That season he turned out twice for South Australia and in the second game, against an Australian Services XI, made a chanceless 112 in a drawn game played over the Christmas-New Year period in Adelaide.

The opportunity to play cricket again must have seemed almost surreal to Bradman and the other leading Australians after the dark years of the war. After all, it wasn't that long before that Singapore had fallen, Darwin been bombed and Japanese submarines forced their way into Sydney Harbour, shelling civilian homes on the surrounding hills. If it wasn't for the bravery of thousands of Australian servicemen and women, the Japanese advances could well have continued. The world had changed, but the fraternity and brotherhood provided by cricket was still alive and the resumption of matches was greeted joyously.

Bradman's playing future was the subject of almost daily debate in the newspapers. 'WILL HE OR WON'T HE?' the banner headlines inquired.

OPPOSITE: the Don was invalided out of the army with fibrositis in June 1941; he was still far from well when representative cricket resumed in 1945

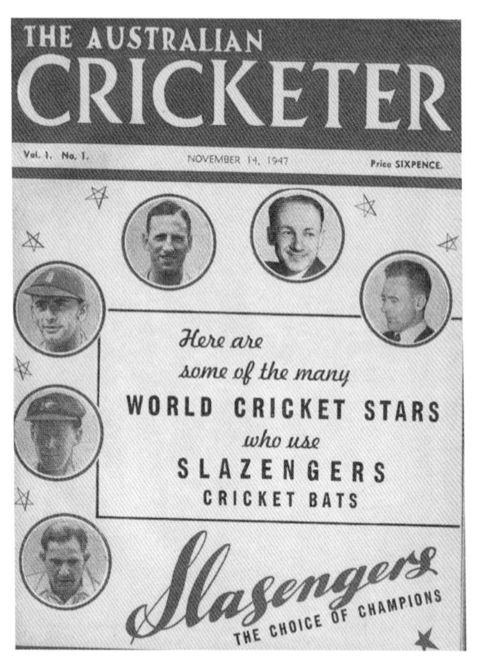

> 'On the field we began to feel sorry he had made a decision to resume his career, but later we were sorry for ourselves as his confidence and form surged back the longer he batted'
>
> *Denis Compton*

His health was gradually on the improve, his century against the Services XI had encouraged him to at least again think about the representative matches. Complicating the issue, however, was his move to establish his own stockbroking firm, Don Bradman & Co., in 1945 after his old boss Harry Hodgetts was bankrupted and gaoled for fraud. Bradman was working abnormally long hours, but knew how much the cricket world wanted him to return to help re-start cricket after the war. His last Australian appearance had been at The Oval, in 1938, when England amassed 900-plus and batted eight full sessions deep into the third day. Both he and Jack Fingleton had been unable to bat because of injury and the Australians were thrashed by an innings. It wasn't lost on Bradman that his old adversary Walter Hammond, England's premier batsman, had been the English captain in this most one-sided of all Ashes encounters. But it probably wasn't until his wife Jessie suggested that it would be nice if their young son John could see him play that he truly resolved to return.

Despite a recurrence of fibrositis in his back during the winter months, his comeback bid gathered momentum when he made two centuries in three games leading into the 1946-47 Test series. He declared himself available and was immediately named captain.

Forty-three-year-old Hammond had returned for a fourth and farewell tour as the MCC's captain and started with a double century in Perth. It was to be one of his few successes, however, as the English team suffered a succession of humiliating reverses.

The Australians of this period were building one of the strongest teams in history, champion sides which were to record a still-unprecedented 25 matches without defeat. Bradman was again to be the cornerstone of the team, alongside some exciting mature-age newcomers including fast bowlers Ray Lindwall, Keith Miller and Bill Johnston.

After an uncertain beginning in his comeback Test at the 'Gabba', Bradman thrilled the spectators with some of his finest strokeplay on his way to 187 and followed later in the summer with 234. It may have been eight years in-between Tests, but he still was a formidable force.

Australia won three of the five Tests; the other two being drawn. Bradman's fortunes could so easily have been different in Brisbane, however, had a contentious catch to England's second slipsman Jack Ikin been allowed. Instead of being out for 28, the Don went on to amass 187 in the finest possible return. Hammond walked past Bradman at the end of the 'Ikin over' and said: 'A fine f...... way to start a series.'

The English were demoralised. 'Every English player thought that it never went within nine inches of the ground,' said another of England's leading players, Bill Edrich. He said Bradman, tense and most unlike his normal self, had played a horizontal bat shot at Bill Voce and slashed the ball shoulder high to Ikin. The Englishmen waited for him to walk and were astonished when he remaining at the crease, staring tight-lipped at the ground, adamant that it was a bump ball. Unwittingly he'd started a trend which today sees umpires under increasing pressure with players refusing to walk, even when it is clear that they are out. A Bradman failure in Brisbane may have caused him to rethink his comeback. Edrich was one of many who thought so. As it was, according to those who had seen him before and after the war, there was simply no comparison in the way he played — yet he was able to maintain and even increase his incredible average.

Bradman made eight centuries in twelve innings during the following season, his last at international level in Australia. Six of the 100s were made against the touring Indians. Included was his 100th century in first-class cricket in his old home town of Sydney. He remains the only Australian to have achieved this milestone.

He may have been past his best but he was still playing at a rare level of competence. He was ruthless all right — and also very proud to have maintained his century habit in front of a new hero-worshipper, his eight-year-old son John.

THE DON IN FIRST-CLASS CRICKET

* Clarrie Grimmett dismissed Bradman ten times in 27 innings. Only Englishman Hedley Verity (also ten) dismissed the Don as often;
* Alan Kippax (seventeen) shared in more century stands with the Don than anyone else, ahead of Stan McCabe and Bill Woodfull (fifteen each) and Bill Brown (twelve);
* The Don hit 44 sixes and 2586 fours in all first-class cricket;
* He averaged 93 in first innings and 100 in second innings;
* The Don's mark of 117 first-class centuries is unequalled among Australians. Next is Darren Lehmann (82) followed by Mark Waugh (81), Justin Langer (80) and Steve Waugh (79).

Australia's First Test team against India, Brisbane, 1947-48.
Back row, left to right, Keith Miller, Bill Johnston, Ernie Toshack. Centre, Ian Johnson, Ray Lindwall, W. H. 'Bill' Jeanes (manager), Don Tallon, Ron Hamence (12th man). Front, Arthur Morris, Bill Brown, Don Bradman, Lindsay Hassett, Colin McCool

'I was forced to admire the cool way Don batted. On one or two occasions, when he was well set, and when he saw me move a fieldsman, he would raise his gloved hand to me in mock salute, and then hit the next ball exactly over the place from which the man had just been moved'

MCC captain Walter Hammond

CHAPTER THIRTEEN

The Invincibles

In going undefeated for all 34 matches in England, the Australian team provided the game's outstanding player with a fairytale farewell ...

It was the happiest tour of all, one in which Australia went unbeaten and new champions emerged. Don Bradman hadn't intended his team to go undefeated all tour. Retaining the Ashes by playing their cricket aggressively and attractively was integral to his touring blueprint. He wanted to bring some relief to war-ravaged England. But as the tour progressed and his Aussies swept from success to success, it was soon obvious that they possessed awesome strength and depth and were as powerful as any Australian team sent to the UK.

Leading into the first Test at Trent Bridge, the Australians had won ten and drawn two of their first twelve games and Bradman was keen to maintain the momentum. Ray Lindwall and Keith Miller provided the launching pad and big Bill Johnston finished them off, the English being bowled out for just 165. Like so many Australian captains at the start of a campaign, Bradman regarded the first days of a new series as the most important. He wanted to make his stamp — and inspire others around him.

Taking his place at his favourite No. 3 position, Bradman saw off the menacing Surrey off-spinner Jim Laker, who had taken 3-22,

TOP: the Don's last tour of England was a triumph from the opening game when he made yet another century at Worcester

OPPOSITE, June, 1948: with opposing captain Norman Yardley at Lord's

TOP, April, 1948: the Australians at Tilbury. They were to enjoy an unparalleled five months' domination. The team's youngest player, 19-year-old Neil Harvey, said that not only were they a champion team but also 'nicer blokes you'd never meet'

OPPOSITE, from top: three cheers for the Don at The Oval; relaxed with King George VI; with Marylebone Cricket Club President and former Governor-General of Australia, Earl Gowrie

and with his deputy Lindsay Hassett shared a matchwinning, three-figure stand for the fifth wicket. On a perfect pitch and in ideal conditions, Bradman made 138, his twenty-eighth Test century and eighteenth against England. He was unusually subdued especially early, refusing to take a risk or to lose patience against Norman Yardley's restrictive field settings and the defensive leg stump line.

At a stumps score of 4-293 — after the Aussies were at one stage 3-121 — it had been yet another Bradman-led recovery. So slow was he at times that he was even slow-handclapped. But Australia won by eight wickets, the first of four wins from five Tests.

At Headingley, in one of the most famous stands of all, he was to make his twenty-ninth and final century as Australia chased 404 on the final day and made them with more than ten minutes to spare.

In what proved to be his last Test innings, at The Oval, the Don was cheered onto the ground by an excited crowd and saluted by Yardley and the English players, who formed a circle around him and gave him three cheers. Arthur Morris was at the non-striker's end and said it was as moving a moment as any he had experienced in cricket and Bradman, clearly affected, was bowled second ball by an Eric Hollies googly which he failed to detect. Had he scored even four runs, it would have given him an average of exactly 100. There was stunned silence as he tucked his bat under his arm and quickly walked away from the wicket. As in Melbourne years earlier, the crowd went absolutely wild with excitement and he left the arena to a standing ovation. Spontaneously the crowd sang: 'For He's a Jolly Good Fellow'.

Inside the rooms, teammate Ron Hamence said: 'Bad luck, Braddles.'

'Oh well,' said the Don, 'it was one of those things, Ronnie.'

Morris said the English crowds were very generous and appreciative of the Australians. 'England had suffered such a devastating few

CENTRE: on his last tour of England the Don scored 11 centuries in 31 innings. BELOW, left: England's captain Norman Yardley watches the Don cut his 40th birthday cake.

BELOW, right: by 1998 nine Invincibles remained. The seven seen here at the MCG are, left to right, Loxton, Morris, Johnston, Ring, Brown, Harvey and Hamence.

LEEDS, July 27.—Australia won the dramatic fourth Test by seven wickets with 13 minutes to spare this afternoon, after being set 404 to make in 345 minutes.

Arthur Morris and Don Bradman put on 301 in a match-winning second-wicket partnership in which they impressively combined sound defence and aggressive enterprise.

Miller was out to Cranston with 15 minutes left, but Neil Harvey, with a drive to the long-on boundary, gave Australia victory. Bradman was 173 not out.

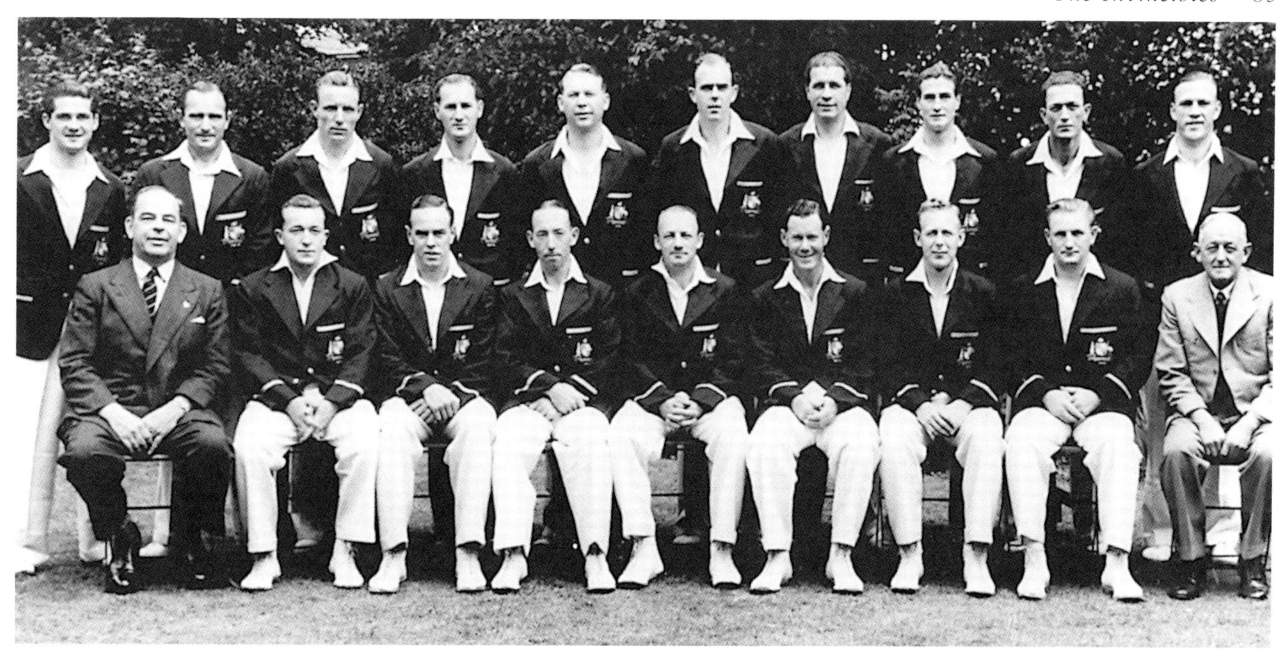

years of war. So much damage had been done. They were looking forward to good cricket and Don gave it to them.'

Teammate Bill Johnston said Bradman's tactical acumen was an underrated factor in Australia's unbeaten run. Bradman commanded universal respect both from the older players who'd played with him before and the younger ones, most of whom worshipped him. 'He treated us as grown men,' said 'Big Bill', 'and we were allowed to do our own thing, as long as we were fit.'

ABOVE: the Don with his Invincibles, back row from left, Neil Harvey, Sid Barnes, Ray Lindwall, Ron Saggers, Doug Ring, Bill Johnston, Ernie Toshack, Keith Miller, Don Tallon, Sam Loxton.
Front, K. E. O. 'Keith' Johnson (manager), Ron Hamence, Ian Johnson, Lindsay Hassett, the Don, Bill Brown, Arthur Morris, Colin McCool, W. 'Bill' Ferguson (scorer).

HAPPY MEMORIES

'People love to remind me that I'm to blame for Bradman not averaging 100 in Test cricket...if I'd only given Bradman the strike and let him hit the winning runs [in the fourth Test at Leeds in 1948]. But how was I to know he was to make a duck in his last Test innings? The ground was chockablock and I can still see him belting past me after I'd hit the winning runs: 'C'mon, son,' he said. 'Let's get out of here.' I had to run as fast as I could to keep up with him and he still beat me to the dressing room gates by ten metres'

Neil Harvey

CHAPTER FOURTEEN

Cricket's ultimate matchwinner

At his peak, Don Bradman was twice as good as anyone else in the game and was directly responsible for at least twelve Australian Test victories...

Don Bradman's on-field influence was extraordinary. He was a colossus in any gathering, a once-in-a-lifetime batsman whose record-breaking impact has been rivalled by only one other, Shane Warne, the sandy-haired spinner from the Melbourne beachside.

As the greatest matchwinner of his time, the Don ruthlessly dominated the finest attacks in the world and became a hero for millions of Australians at a time when the Great Depression was biting and one in three were out of work. The young Don offered fresh hope to the young and the old alike. They revelled in his astonishing run sprees and marvelled at his concentration and focus. He was all but unstoppable; no bowler, or captain, had a conventional answer to quell his supremacy.

The Second World War and his own on-going health problems reduced his career to just 52 Tests over a twenty-year period but he was a champion virtually from his first appearances.

Australia lost only two of eight Ashes series in which he figured: in 1928-29, when he was just starting and was inexplicably dropped after a landslide of a loss in his debut Test in Brisbane; and in 1932-33, when England's win-at-any-cost captain Douglas Jardine directed his fast bowlers to bowl straight at the Australian batsmen, tactics which enraged the players and public and temporarily endangered Empire relations.

OPPOSITE: bowlers were intimidated by the presence of Australia's two record-breakers, the Don and Bill 'Puddin' Ponsford

TESTS THE DON 'WON'

His scores	
1-Melbourne, 1928-29	123 & 37 not out
2-Lord's, 1930	254 & 1
3-Melbourne, 1931-32	2 & 167
4-Adelaide, 1931-32	299 not out
5-Melbourne, 1932-33	0 & 103 not out
6-The Oval, 1934	244 & 77
7-Melbourne, 1936-37	13 & 270
8-Adelaide, 1936-37	26 & 212
9-Leeds, 1938	103 & 16
10-Melbourne, 1947-48	132 & 127 not out
11-Nottingham, 1948	138 & 0
12-Leeds, 1948	33 & 173 not out

June, 1948: evading Englishman Alec Bedser's renowned leg-trap at Lord's

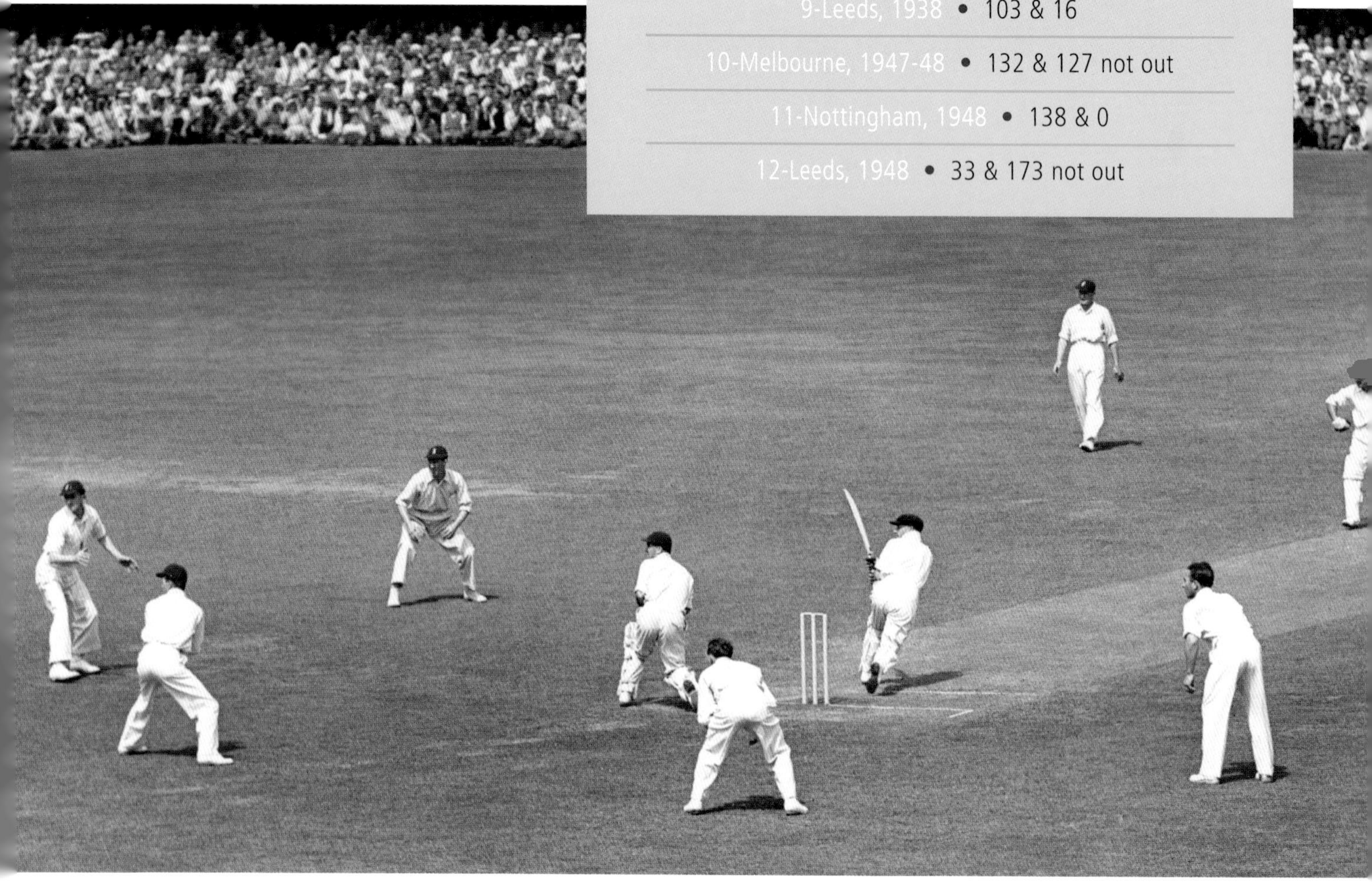

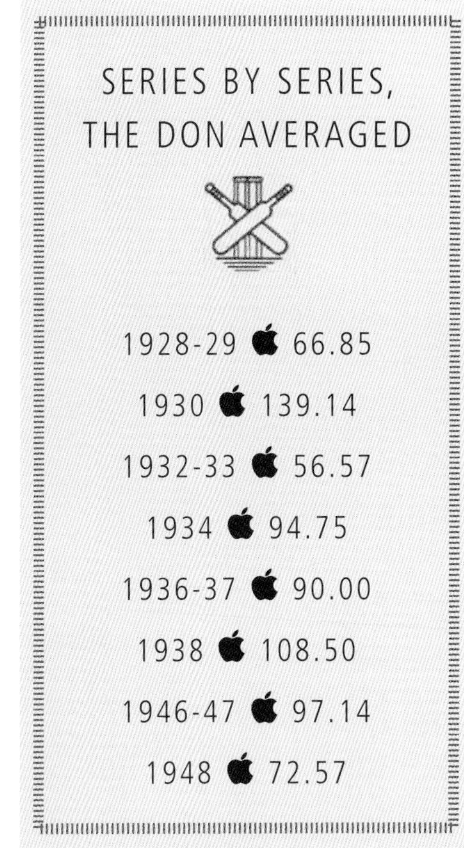
SERIES BY SERIES, THE DON AVERAGED

1928-29 66.85

1930 139.14

1932-33 56.57

1934 94.75

1936-37 90.00

1938 108.50

1946-47 97.14

1948 72.57

Statisticians claim Bradman was directly responsible for twelve Australian wins in his 52 Tests, at a rate of one every four Test matches, a superior strike-rate well ahead of everyone else, including Warne. So commanding and so formidable was his presence that English teams could only hope, rather than expect to win.

In the last 47 of his 52 Tests, the Don never scored a century for a losing side. Ten of his centuries came in matches Australia won by an innings. The most revered of these were his 232 at The Oval in 1930 and his 234 at Sydney in 1946-47. His double century against the Indians in Adelaide in 1947-48 was another game he dominated. It was the highest score in Australia's mammoth 674, the Indians being swept aside by an innings and sixteen runs.

Bradman won nine of these twelve Tests before turning 30. Teammate Neil Harvey, Australia's finest batsman of the '50s, said Bradman was still extraordinarily good after the war.

'He must have been out of this world beforehand,' he said.

DON BRADMAN TESTIMONIAL

SPORTS PARADE

Under the Auspices of the Victorian Cricket Association.

In the presence of His Excellency Major-General Sir Winston Dugan, G.C.M.G., C.B., D.S.O., Governor of Victoria.

MELBOURNE TOWN HALL

Friday, 3rd December, 1948

The Don Bradman Testimonial Edition of "Kia-Ora Sports Parade" will be broadcast from 3KZ, Melbourne, and a nation-wide network. Overseas transmissions, to all countries, will be from Radio Australia.

SOUVENIR PROGRAMME 6d. Nº 166

CHAPTER FIFTEEN

In love with Melbourne

No one has made more Test 100s in Melbourne than Don Bradman...

So rousing and prolonged was the ovation for a twenty-year-old Don Bradman when he made his first Test century at his favourite Melbourne Cricket Ground in 1928-29 that England's fast bowler Harold Larwood sat down at the head of his run-up and waited for the commotion to subside. 'I wish you could have been here to hear it,' Bradman later wrote to his fiancée Jessie.

It began a remarkable run of success which saw the Don make nine centuries and average 128 in his eleven Tests at cricket's Colosseum.

Given that he didn't bat in one match through injury and had to retire hurt in another when well set, his record could have been even more remarkable. England's champion Len Hutton said the Don at his best was worth three batsmen to any team. The Don won five games in Melbourne virtually himself.

At no other ground was he more prolific or as menacing. His 270 batting down the list in the thrilling 1936-37 encounter revived Australia after it had lost each of the first two rain-affected Tests of the summer. World record crowds of more than 60,000 fans streamed into the ground for six days in a row to revel in Australia's Bradman-inspired comeback.

OPPOSITE, December, 1948: the Don takes the field for the last time at the Melbourne Cricket Ground during his testimonial match where he scored his 117th and last first-class century

The Don and Jack Fingleton added 346 in this match, a monumental stand and the highest of the six century stands he shared at the MCG. In 1931-32 against the visiting Springboks, his 167 included a century in 98 minutes, the fastest 100 in Tests at the MCG in the twentieth century.

THE DON IN TESTS

	Matches	Inns	NO	HS	Runs	Ave	100s
At the MCG	11	17	4	270	1671	128.53	9
Overall	52	80	10	334	6996	99.94	29

HIS 100s IN MELBOURNE

112 v England, third Test (second innings), 1928-29

123 v England, fifth Test (first innings), 1928-29

152 v West Indies, fourth Test (first innings), 1930-31

167 v South Africa, third Test (second innings), 1931-32

103* v England, second Test (second innings), 1932-33

270 v England, third Test (second innings), 1936-37

169 v England, fifth Test (first innings), 1936-37

132 v India, third Test (first innings), 1947-48

127* v India, third Test (second innings), 1947-48

HIS 100-RUN STANDS AT THE MCG

Second wicket

274 – with Bill Woodfull, v South Africa, 1931-32

156 – with Bill Woodfull, v West Indies, 1930-31

Third wicket

249 – with Stan McCabe, v England, 1936-37

169 – with Lindsay Hassett, v India, 1947-48

Fifth wicket

223 – with Arthur Morris, v India, 1947-48

Sixth wicket

346 – with Jack Fingleton, v England, 1936-37

THE DON IN FIRST-CLASS CRICKET

	Matches	Inns	NO	HS	Runs	Ave	100s
At the MCG	29	47	8	357	4024	103.17	19
Overall	234	338	43	452*	28,067	95.14	117

THE DON'S TEST RECORD, GROUND BY GROUND

In Australia	Matches	Ave	100s
Adelaide	7	107.77	3
Brisbane (Exhibition)	2	80.66	1
Brisbane ('Gabba)	5	105.14	3
Melbourne	11	128.53	9
Sydney	8	58.58	2
In England			
Headingley	4	192.60	4
Lord's	4	78.71	2
Old Trafford	3	27.00	-
The Oval	4	138.25	2
Trent Bridge	4	75.14	3

* Australians unless otherwised denoted

MOST TEST 100S AT THE MCG

9 • Don Bradman

6 • Matthew Hayden

5 • Jack Hobbs (Eng.)

4 • Allan Border, Greg Chappell, Bill Lawry, Herbert Sutcliffe (Eng.)

3 • Warwick Armstrong, Ian Chappell, Colin Cowdrey (Eng.), Neil Harvey, Ricky Ponting, Ian Redpath, Steve Waugh, Bill Woodfull

December, 1948: teams for the Don's testimonial match at the MCG.
Back row, left to right, Vic Raymer, Ray Lindwall, Doug Ring, Geff Noblet, Bill Johnston, Keith Miller, Don Tallon, Wally Langdon.
Middle, R. 'Ron' Wright (umpire), Bruce Dooland, Merv Harvey, Len Johnson, W. H. 'Bill' Jeanes (secretary, SACA), H. 'Harry' Brereton (secretary, VCA), Sam Loxton, Colin McCool, Sid Barnes, A. 'Andy' Barlow (umpire).
Seated, Ian Johnson, Arthur Morris, Ken Meuleman, Bill Brown, the Don, Lindsay Hassett, Neil Harvey, Ron Saggers, Ron Hamence

CHAPTER SIXTEEN

Jessie

Don and Jessie Bradman were to be married for 65 years, Bradman describing their marriage as 'the best partnership' of his life...

Don Bradman decided at twelve that he would marry Jessie Menzies, a dairy farmer's daughter from nearby Glenquarry. But he was too shy to tell her.

She was fifteen months younger than Don and as a child she used to stay with the Bradman family during the school week and attend the local Bowral school. He'd carry her books to school across the local cricket ground.

Interviewed by Channel 9's Ray Martin in 1996, Bradman admitted he had fallen in love with Jessie the very first day she came to stay. 'I remember the day well as I had been sent down the street to buy some groceries and I ran into the doctor's car on my bike and had an accident,' he said. 'He had to take me home. I had my nose all cut and scratches all over my face. And when I got home, she (Jessie) was there at the door, having just been delivered by her father. She was going to stay with us and go to school for twelve months. And we went to school together every day for the rest of the year. That was when I fell in love with her, that very first day.

'I don't think she fell in love with me until much later because I was a terrible sight the day she saw me.'

OPPOSITE: the Don and Jessie Bradman in January, 1994. She was a grand beauty, with wavy auburn hair and deep blue eyes

Jessie was a grand beauty, with wavy auburn hair and deep blue

Mrs. Bradman's Hobby

The life of a first-class cricketer's wife is not all it may seem on the evidence of an interview with Mrs. Bradman on her hobbies.

A cricketer's wife, apparently, has little time for such things, she is so fully occupied in sharing her husband's trials, as well as his triumphs.

"I have had only one hobby in the last two years," she confesses, "and that is looking after Don. In the face of a barrage of criticism he kept a smiling face to the world, and I was with him through it all."

Through his breakdown Mrs. Bradman nursed her husband so well that his friends say he might never have seen the cricket season through if it had not been for her care and attention. Then, during the season just concluded, Mrs. Bradman, day after day, jotted down notes to refresh the memory of her husband, who was to write and broadcast at night after a strenuous day in the field.

—"The Herald."

eyes. She was friendly, outgoing, a fine athlete and also a noted horsewoman.

Bradman proposed in 1930 and wanted to marry her immediately, but Jessie said Don should go to England with his cricket and see if he felt the same way on his return. They were engaged in 1931 and married in 1932 at St Paul's Anglican Church in Burwood, just around the corner from where Jessie first lived when she came to Sydney to work.

Their marriage in April 1932 created a minor sensation, fans knocking down barricades to catch a glimpse of the beautiful bride and her famous husband. Don's brother Vic was best man and Jessie's brother Roy a groomsman.

They were to enjoy an extended honeymoon on the *Niagara* in the USA and Canada, Bradman having agreed to join Arthur Mailey's private tour, on the proviso that Jessie could come too. They were to have three children, Ross (born 1936), who was to live for less than 36 hours, John (born 1939) and Shirley (1941). John Bradman suffered polio in his early teens before making a complete recovery. He was a schoolboy athletics champion and also a fine cricketer, good enough to score a century in his last year at school. He studied law and became a barrister.

Shirley was born with cerebral palsy and for years worked with handicapped children and the blind. The family's home was in

Holden St, Kensington Park, a quiet street in a comfortable inner-city Adelaide suburb.

Jessie was not only a wife and a mother, she helped the Don write some of his speeches and worked, too, as his part-time book-keeper when he was establishing Don Bradman & Co. During the war, after his fibrositis forced his premature discharge from the Army, she nursed him and even shaved him. She was caring, reliable and selfless.

The pair were extraordinarily close and after her death, from cancer, in 1997, Bradman said he'd never known an Adelaide winter to be as cold. He never truly recovered from her passing. He said his partnership with Jessie was by far the best of his life. She was the finest woman he ever met.

A MINOR MIRACLE

The Don was digging in his vegetable garden in Kensington one day when he uncovered a small ring, Jessie's much-loved engagement ring, which had long been missing, presumed lost. It is now a favourite family heirloom.

OPPOSITE, top right: Jessie and the Don have film-star appeal in Wellington, New Zealand, 1932.

ABOVE: during their extended honeymoon in the USA and Canada in 1932.

LEFT: together at the Don's beloved Bowral in 1989

CHAPTER SEVENTEEN

Life after cricket

Cricket was like a room with the light off when the Don retired. But the Don's contribution as a leader and an administrator were to continue for years...

Don Bradman was knighted for his services to cricket on New Year's Day 1949, but his participation and passion for the game was only starting, his service to cricket off the field every bit as strong as it was on.

Twice he served three-year terms as chairman of the Australian Board of Control for international cricket and was influential in stamping out throwing. He also assisted in selecting Australian teams from 1936 to 1971, missing only one season 1952-53, when his son, John, developed polio. As an administrator on South Australian Cricket Association committees spanning 51 years from 1935-36 to 1985-86, the Don attended 1713 meetings!

Having originally worked in Adelaide for stockbroker Harry Hodgetts, Bradman established his own stockbroking and investment business, Don Bradman & Co., before retiring in June, 1954 at the age of 45. In the next 30 years he was to take up more than a dozen directorships with companies including Kelvinator, F. H. Faulding & Co and Argo Investments. He was persuaded to play a few games of cricket in his 40s, most notably in the annual St Peter's first XI v The Fathers fixture when he was caught and bowled by son John but not before he had made equal top score of 22. Historian Alf James says rather than retire the Don skied a ball deliberately straight up in the air for John to catch.

OPPOSITE: Jessie and Don with John and Shirley on the Don's return from England in 1948

His last game, was for the Prime Minister's XI against the touring MCC at Manuka Oval, Canberra in 1962-63. He made four before being bowled by England's Brian Statham. Overjoyed by the nostalgia of it all, one journalist wrote: 'This was the day of Sir Donald, the day Bradman came back to cricket. And in cricket it rated as would a reappearance of Michelangelo in the art world or Keats among the poets.'

In 1972 John told him he was changing his name (to Bradsen) to escape the non-stop public scrutiny engendered by his being the son of the most famous cricketer of them all. Bradman claimed it was one of the saddest days of his life. It wasn't until January 2000 when his father was ill and bedridden that John reverted to his surname of birth.

The Don continued to travel extensively into his mid-60s, before being told by doctors to restrict his activities and travel, for health reasons. He was to undertake only a few select public speaking engagements afterwards and even fewer interviews. One notable speech was at the Centenary Test dinner in Melbourne where hundreds came from interstate and overseas for Test cricket's 100th birthday celebrations. So huge was the Don's mail that for years the Adelaide Post Office would deliver twice a day to the Bradman household in Holden St, Kensington Park. He regularly received up to 400 letters each week and answered them all well into his '80s, before the death of Lady Bradman.

In 1979 he was made a Companion of the Order of Australia, an honour ranking even higher than his knighthood.

THE FATHERS

GH BLACK	b. Black	4
RD BLANDY	run out	2
TW WALL	c. Moorhouse, b. Blandy	0
KCC LAHEY	retired	20
TK MOORHOUSE	retired	22
HHH BEGG	c. Clayton, b. Begg	8
Sir Donald BRADMAN	c. & b. Bradman	22
TB BRUCE	b. Symons	17
AAK GIFFORD	c. sub. (Watson), b. Symons	13
MC CLAYTON	not out	11
ES LING	c. Birks, b. Ling	4
Extras		5
Total		**128**
Fall : not known		

	O	M	R	W
Black			3	1
Blandy			18	1
Begg			12	1
Bradman			27	1
			14	2

OPPOSITE, from top left: Bradman the selector, with Jack Ryder in Melbourne; with England captain Len Hutton in 1954-55; with his son John; saying thank-you to Melburnians in 1948 for their support

LEFT: the scorecard from the 1951 The Fathers v St Peter's (school) First XI match where the Don made top score before being caught and bowled by his son John

BELOW: passing on some tips at the Adelaide Oval nets to young South Australians Neil Dansie, left, and Bob Lee

SIR DONALD BRADMAN, A.C.

2 HOLDEN STREET,
KENSINGTON PARK,
SOUTH AUSTRALIA 5068

4.8.83

Dear Ken,

I'm sorry to disappoint you but I do not feel that my involvement in cricket or observations of matches make me qualified to judge the top 4 cricketers in the world therefore I am unwilling to commit my views to public scrutiny.

Yours faithfully

Don Bradman

MOST SEASONS AS AN AUSTRALIAN TEST SELECTOR

26 • Sir Donald Bradman, Jack Ryder

13 • Neil Harvey, Trevor Hohns, Phil Ridings, Dudley Seddon

11 • Sam Loxton

His favourite indulgence, outside his grandkids, was golf. He played at Adelaide's Kooyonga club, playing off scratch within a year of his international retirement. He was a regular 'A' grade pennant player, too, and into his mid-80s regularly beat his age. Having to give up the game was one of his greatest regrets.

Some say that had the Don been more proactive in encouraging more lucrative salaries for Australian players in the '60s and '70s, World Series Cricket would never have occurred. His then-secret meeting with Kerry Packer in early 1979 helped broker a peace deal which saw WSC disbanded and Channel 9 finally win the exclusive television rights it had sought years before. When Trevor Chappell bowled the infamous underarm ball to end a one-day international at the Melbourne Cricket Ground in 1981, the phone in the match office rang. It was the Don. He couldn't believe the spirit of cricket had been so violated.

The Don loved returning to Bowral in the NSW southern highlands where he played all his junior cricket and had met Jessie Menzies, his wife of 65 years. The first stage of the Bradman Museum opened in 1989, the Don and Lady Bradman in attendance.

Among the few interviews he granted in his final years was with

March 1949: the Don's last innings in interstate ranks; bowled by Bill Johnston for 30 at the Adelaide Oval

Norman May for an ABC series entitled *The Don Declares* around the time of his 75th birthday. In 1996 he gave his last 'public' interview, with Channel 9's Ray Martin. His fee of $A1 million was donated directly to the Bradman Foundation.

A gala black tie dinner was held at the Adelaide Oval in honour of his 90th birthday in 1998, Indian batting great Sachin Tendulkar and the Australian spin-bowling legend Shane Warne among the guests. The Don did not attend but met the pair privately at his home, Tendulkar calling it 'a thrill of a lifetime'.

Years earlier, Bradman had been watching Tendulkar bat on television and told Lady Bradman that Tendulkar, with all his focus and flair, was the one who most reminded him of himself at the crease.

Among countless honours accorded him later in life was his inclusion in the Australian cricket Team of the Century in 2000-01. Fellow members were Allan Border, Greg Chappell, Neil Harvey, Ian Healy, Dennis Lillee, Ray Lindwall, Keith Miller, Arthur Morris, Bill O'Reilly, Bill Ponsford and Shane Warne.

LEFT: the Don at the Adelaide Oval in 1984 during the celebrations for one hundred years' Test cricket at that beautiful ground

ABOVE: Sachin Tendulkar's focus and flair caused the Don to comment that Tendulkar was the batsman who most reminded him of himself

CHAPTER EIGHTEEN

Interlude

TWENTY-SIX QUIZ QUESTIONS

1 • In which NSW country town was Don Bradman born on August 27, 1908?

2 • On which ground did Bradman make his first and last first-class appearances?

3 • What was the given name of his mother?

4 • Who was Bradman's vice-captain on the Invincibles tour of England in 1948?

5 • Which club team did Bradman represent in his initial years in Sydney?

6 • In 1932, the Don married his childhood sweetheart – a marriage lasting 65 years. What was his wife's name?

7 • In which suburb in the St George district of Sydney did Bradman live from 1928 to 1932?

8 • Against which country did Bradman make his highest Test score in Australia of 299 not out?

9 • Who was England's captain in the Don's first Ashes series as skipper in 1936-37?

10 • Who is the chairman of the Bradman Foundation and the Bradman Museum?

11 • How many appearances did Bradman make in his first-class career?

ABOVE: the waxwork Don, a fixture for many years at London's Madame Tussauds

OPPOSITE: Englishman Alec Bedser delivered the best ball the Don ever faced, a leg-cutter that bowled him in Adelaide, 1946-47

BELOW: entertaining at home with visitors Mignon Laurenti and Larry Adler

BOTTOM: at the piano, with 'Chuck' Fleetwood-Smith standing next to him and Arthur Chipperfield

12 • What was the name of Jessie and Don's first son who died soon after he was born in 1936?

13 • Who was the Victorian slow bowler Bradman lifted for three 6s in an over at the Sydney Cricket Ground in 1933-34?

14 • Who bowled the last ball the Don faced in Test cricket?

15 • What colour is the Sir Donald Bradman rose?

16 • What is its fragrance?

17 • What is Sir Donald's connection with the song *Every Day is a Rainbow Day For Me*?

18 • What was Bradman's occupation after he moved from Sydney to Adelaide in 1934?

19 • What was the title of the autobiography the Don published in 1950?

20 • In 1972 he described an innings at the MCG as the best he had seen. Who was the batsman?

21 • Who was the actor who played the role of Bradman in the 1984 television series 'Bodyline'?

22 • Don Bradman once called this man the best administrator in Australia — before lunch. Who was he referring to?

23 • Who played most Tests alongside the Don?

24 • What was the name of Don and Jessie's daughter?

25 • Name two who were accorded the rank as being 'the next Bradman'?

26 • What was the Don's middle name?

AND SOME HARDER ONES

1 • Who was the player the Don defeated for the 1939 South Australian squash championship?

2 • Who was the legendary American harmonica player who 'jammed' with the Don (on piano) at his Adelaide home in 1957?

3 • In which Adelaide inner suburb did the Don live?

FORTY-THREE BRADMAN FACTS

1 • The young Don was twelve when he first visited the Sydney Cricket Ground and saw Charlie Macartney, cricket's 'Governor-General', make 170 against England. 'I shall never be satisfied,' vowed the young Don, 'until I play on this ground.'

2 • Having left school at fourteen, his first job was as a clerk for a real estate company, Deer & Westbrook in Bong Bong St, Bowral.

3 • For two years, at the ages of fifteen and sixteen, Bradman played

more tennis than cricket and was a Country Week representative.

4 • He was also a table tennis player of note and in 1925 at the Kangaloon Hall defeated the southern highlands table tennis champion Oscar Bunt 21/18 in the final.

5 • He was just seventeen when he made his first triple century: 300 for Bowral against Moss Vale for the Tom Mack Cup, the final lasting five Saturdays.

6 • His NSW teammates called him 'Braddles' and on tour would ask him to play tunes on the piano.

7 • On 30 November 1928, the young Don became Australian Test player No.124 when first stepping onto Brisbane's old Exhibition Ground for the opening Test against England.

8 • The *Cooktown Independent* in north Queensland declared Bradman dead, from dysentery, in December 1931: 'Australia today mourns the loss of the greatest batsman the world has ever seen,' it said. In his autobiography, Bradman quipped: 'Thank goodness it was only the *Cooktown Independent*, but it just goes to show that things can really happen in the world without our knowledge.'

9 • Having enjoyed a record-breaking first tour of England, Bradman recorded two piano pieces *Old Fashioned Locket* and *Our Bungalow of Dreams* ('78 rpm) for Columbia Records.

10 • The Don bowled occasional leg-breaks and took two wickets in Tests: West Indian Ivan Barrow in 1930-31 and England's Walter Hammond in 1932-33. Barrow was lbw and Hammond bowled. Both dismissals came in Adelaide. In 1938, at The Oval, the last time he bowled in a Test, Bradman turned an ankle while bowling and had to be carried from the field. He was unable to bat.

11 • In 1936, the Don rejected an offer of £3000 to write, rather than playing in the Ashes Tests ... at the time his annual salary was £6000, plus some money from cricket.

12 • Cheerful Englishman Bill Andrews dined out for years on his success, in 1938, against the Don. 'Shake the hand that bowled Bradman,' he'd often say as a way of introduction. Andrews even titled his memoirs *The Hand That Bowled Bradman*. And how many did the Don make before being bowled that day? 202!

13 • Indian Gogumai Kishenchand played only five Tests and averaged less than ten but is forever linked with Don Bradman as he was bowling in Sydney, complete with his cap on, when the Don took a single to advance from 99 to 100 and record his 100th first-class century during his last full Australian season in 1947-48. Kishenchand hadn't previ-

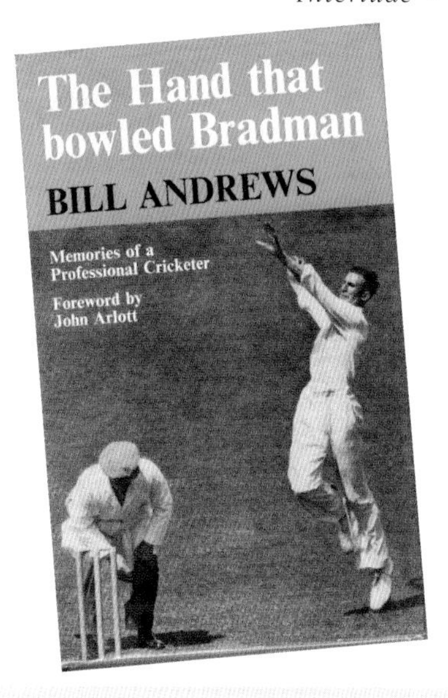

ANSWERS

1. Cootamundra. **2.** Adelaide Oval.
3. Emily. **4.** Lindsay Hassett.
5. St George. **6.** Jessie. **7.** Rockdale.
8. South Africa 1931-32.
9. G. O. 'Gubby' Allen. **10.** Ian Craig.
11. 234. **12.** Ross.
13. L. O'B. 'Chuck' Fleetwood-Smith.
14. Englishman Eric Hollies.
15. Cricket ball red. **16.** Apple-scented.
17. He recorded it.
18. Stockbroker. **19.** 'Farewell to Cricket'.
20. Garry Sobers. **21.** Gary Sweet.
22. Bob Radford. **23.** Stan McCabe.
24. Shirley. **25.** Ian Craig & Norman O'Neill.
26. George.

AND THE HARDER ONES

1. Donald Turnbull. **2.** Larry Adler.
3. Kensington Park.

THIRTEEN BRADMAN NICKNAMES

1 - Braddles

2 - Dynamite Don

3 - Cricket's Walter Lindrum

4 Goldie

5 - The Antipodean Slugger

6 - The Babe Ruth of Cricket

7 - The Boy from Bowral

8 - The Don

9 - George

10 - The Knight

11 The Little Fella

12 - The Wizard of the Willow

13 - The Darling of Australia

ously bowled a ball in Australia and sent down just three overs for the entire tour. Bradman rarely showed much emotion at the crease, but on this occasion did a joyful skip and pumped his fist in excitement before being congratulated by his partner, Keith Miller.

14 • The Don lost eight tosses out of nine as Australia's Ashes captain in England. He called 'heads' every time.

15 • As Australian captain, the Don averaged 101, compared with 98 previously as a player. In first-class cricket, he averaged 98 as captain and 91 as non-captain.

16 • The Don was involved in seven Test run outs, but was run out only once himself, by Englishman Jack Hobbs from cover point in the Adelaide Test of 1928-29.

The other partners run out were: – Bill Woodfull and Stan McCabe during Bradman's 152 against the West Indies in 1930-31 in Melbourne; – Alan Kippax and 'Pud' Thurlow in Adelaide in 1931-32 during the Don's record 299 not out; – Bert Ironmonger in the MCG Bodyline Test during Bradman's 103 not out; – And Ross Gregory in Adelaide in 1936-37 when Bradman made 212.

During Bradman's 299 not out, Bert Oldfield should have been run out, too, when the Don was on 199, but the throw from the inner ring was wide.

17 • Only fifteen bowlers ever bowled the Don for a duck, seven in Tests, namely: West Indian Herman Griffith, Sydney; 1930-31 and Englishmen Bill Bowes, Melbourne, 1932-33; G. O. 'Gubby' Allen, Brisbane, 1936-37; Bill Voce, Sydney 1936-37; Alec Bedser, Adelaide, 1946-47; Bedser again, Trent Bridge, 1948; and Eric Hollies, The Oval, 1948. The Bowes dismissal was the only time he was out first ball in Tests.

18 • It remains the best ball the Don ever faced...the leg-cutter from England's Alec Bedser which bowled him in Adelaide in 1946-47. 'It must have come three quarters of the way straight on the off stump then suddenly dipped to pitch on the leg stump, only to turn off the pitch and hit the middle and off stumps,' Bradman later wrote. Like the iconic Sydney Barnes, Bedser's leg-cutter was unplayable on responsive surfaces. With his accuracy and stamina he was a captain's dream. While Bedser had his moments against the Don, most notably in the early Tests in 1948 when Bradman was caught three times by Len Hutton at leg slip, he was never his 'bunny'. In all matches against English attacks including Bedser, Bradman averaged 92.

19 • The fastest spell Bradman claimed he ever faced was from the

Golfing at Sudbury GC, Middlesex, England, 1934. Bill Ponsford is nearest the camera. The Don played golf into his late 80s, and in 1988, aged 80, shot 76 off the back tees at Kooyonga in South Australia. Then in 1994, at 86, he won six club events and had his handicap lowered

Barambah Aboriginal bowler Eddie Gilbert, pictured right, in Brisbane in 1931. The Don made a sixth-ball duck and said never before had he faced such a withering burst of sheer speed.

20 • The Don hit just six sixes during his 80 innings and 52 Tests. Five came against England and one against India. His first six in first-class cricket came in his sixth first-class season.

21 • Bradman was never dismissed in the 90s in a Test match and only six times in 295 first-class innings (at 91, 92, 96, 97 twice and 98).

22 • Thirty-seven of the Don's 117 centuries were of 200-plus, including a highest at Test level of 334.

23 • Bradman averaged approximately 63 runs per 100 balls in Test innings in Australia. It's impossible to be totally sure as scorebooks for the West Indian and South African series in the early '30s are missing. Scorebooks, however, have survived from all Ashes Tests, where the Don tended to bat more slowly. He also batted a little more slowly after the Second World War and the books are complete for that period. Statistician Charles Davis says the Don's overall scoring rate in England was 58.6 runs per 100 balls.

24 • The Don's incredible record in Melbourne included nine centuries in eleven Tests. In one of the MCG Tests, against the 1931-32 South Africans, he was unable to bat, having twisted his ankle in the dressing rooms just as the Australians were about to go out to field. According to one journalist the Don had been 'skylarking'. Bradman claimed the injury was caused merely 'from jumping down from a form' when his sprigs caught in the coir matting, causing him to twist his ankle. Australian physician Dr Ramsay Mailer advised Bradman not to bat or field on the first day and the game was to finish in less than two.

25 • The most celebrated of the Don's centuries in Melbourne was his unbeaten 103 in the second innings of the bodyline Test, the one in which he'd fallen first ball in the first innings. When the last man, St Kilda, Victoria and Australian No. 11 Bert 'Dainty' Ironmonger,

TOP: Bradman Oval at Bowral, NSW, the home of the Bradman Museum

ABOVE: the Aboriginal fast bowler Eddie Gilbert dismissed the Don for a sixth-ball duck in 1931 came to the wicket, the Don was 98. 'Don't worry, son, I won't let you down,' said Ironmonger. Old Bert had failed to score a run in 45 of his 127 first-class innings, but he duly lasted the final two balls of an over from Walter Hammond to once again allow Bradman the strike for his century.

26 • In January 1937, Bradman made an MCG-best 270, including a record 192 runs on the fourth day, surpassing Clem Hill's 182 on the opening day of the Melbourne Test in 1897-98.

The Don didn't bowl much, especially in later years, but had a hat-trick to his name when he took six wickets in one memorable eight-ball over at Mount Tolmie in Victoria, Canada, in 1932

27 • During the war, Bradman volunteered for the Royal Australian Air Force before subsequently transferring to the Army as a supervisor of physical education. For some time he was based at Frankston, 40 km south of Melbourne.

28 • Bradman made two-thirds of his Ashes Test runs for Australia from the No.3 position, where he averaged 93 runs an innings. He tended to dominate anywhere he batted. At No.7 for example, he averaged 162.

29 • In 1947 Bowral's Glebe Park was renamed Bradman Oval in honour of the Don's mighty career.

30 • In his final innings at The Oval, in 1948, he was bowled for 0 by an Eric Hollies googly, having minutes before been given three cheers by the English team led by Norman Yardley. The crowd joined the players in singing, *For He's a Jolly Good Fellow*. Later it was revealed he had needed to score only four runs to finish with a career Test average of 100.

31 • The Don's win-loss record from 52 Tests was 30/12 with 10 matches drawn.

32 • After retirement, the Don was a regular visitor to England and covered two Ashes tours for English newspapers in 1953 and 1956. Sitting next to him in the press box at Headingley during the Coronation Year tour was Douglas Jardine, his old bodyline tour adversary, who was also writing for the London *Daily Mail*.

33 • Bradman rejected an invitation from the Australian Labor Party to enter politics, saying he didn't like the lifestyle. Previously Prime Minister Sir Robert Menzies had asked if he would be interested in the position of Australian High Commissioner in London. At one time, too, he applied for the job of secretary at the Melbourne Cricket Club, but missed out to Melburnian and former Australian batsman Vernon Ransford.

34 • Australian actor Gary Sweet, a keen club standard batsman with a career-best score of 76, played the role of Bradman in the acclaimed

TV mini-series *Bodyline* in the late '80s. He met the Don before filming and said his recall and sharpness of mind were extraordinary.

35 • The church bell at St Phillip's in Sydney was rung 6996 times for Sir Donald and Lady Jessie's 60th wedding anniversary in 1992.

36 • The ABC's post office boxes nationally are 9994, after the Don's batting average.

37 • In 2000 Bradman was named the No.1 player among the five *Wisden* Cricketers of the Century.

38 • After the Don's death was announced, in February 2001, flags were lowered to half mast all over the country as a sign of respect for the greatest Australian sportsmen of them all.

39 • A three-metre bronze statue of the Don, by sculptor Louis Laumen, right, unveiled at the Melbourne Cricket Ground in 2002 was the first honouring Australian cricketing icons. It depicts Bradman raising his bat acknowledging the applause of the crowd. Other cricketers to be sculpted are Keith Miller, Dennis Lillee and Bill Ponsford.

40 • Lauda Air named its new Boeing 777 Donald Bradman in 2002. It services the Melbourne–Sydney–Vienna routes.

41 • Melbourne-based author Roland Perry interviewed the Don about his Best XI of all time and published it in *Bradman's Best*, after the Don's death in 2001. In batting order the team was: Barry Richards (South Africa), Arthur Morris (Australia), Don Bradman (Australia), Sachin Tendulkar (India), Garry Sobers (West Indies), Don Tallon (Australia), Ray Lindwall (Australia), Dennis Lillee (Australia), Alec Bedser (England), Bill O'Reilly (Australia), Clarrie Grimmett (Australia).

42 • Indian champion Sachin Tendulkar was discussing the passion for cricket and the Don in India with an Australian friend. 'Do you know who 99.9 per cent of the kids want to be?' Tendulkar asked.

'Sachin Tendulkar, Gavaskar…'

'No.'

'Who'

'Sir Donald Bradman…and so would I.'

43 • Five of the Don's most-famous bats are on permanent loan to the State Library of South Australia in Adelaide as part of their Bradman Exhibition: the bat he used when making 334 at Leeds (1930); his first triple century bat (340 not out for NSW v Victoria in 1928-29) his 100th 100 bat (for an Australian XI v India, 1947-48); his 452 not out bat (NSW v Queensland, 1929-30); and his first Test century bat, an Alan Kippax autographed *Extra Special*, from his first Ashes battles (in 1928-29).

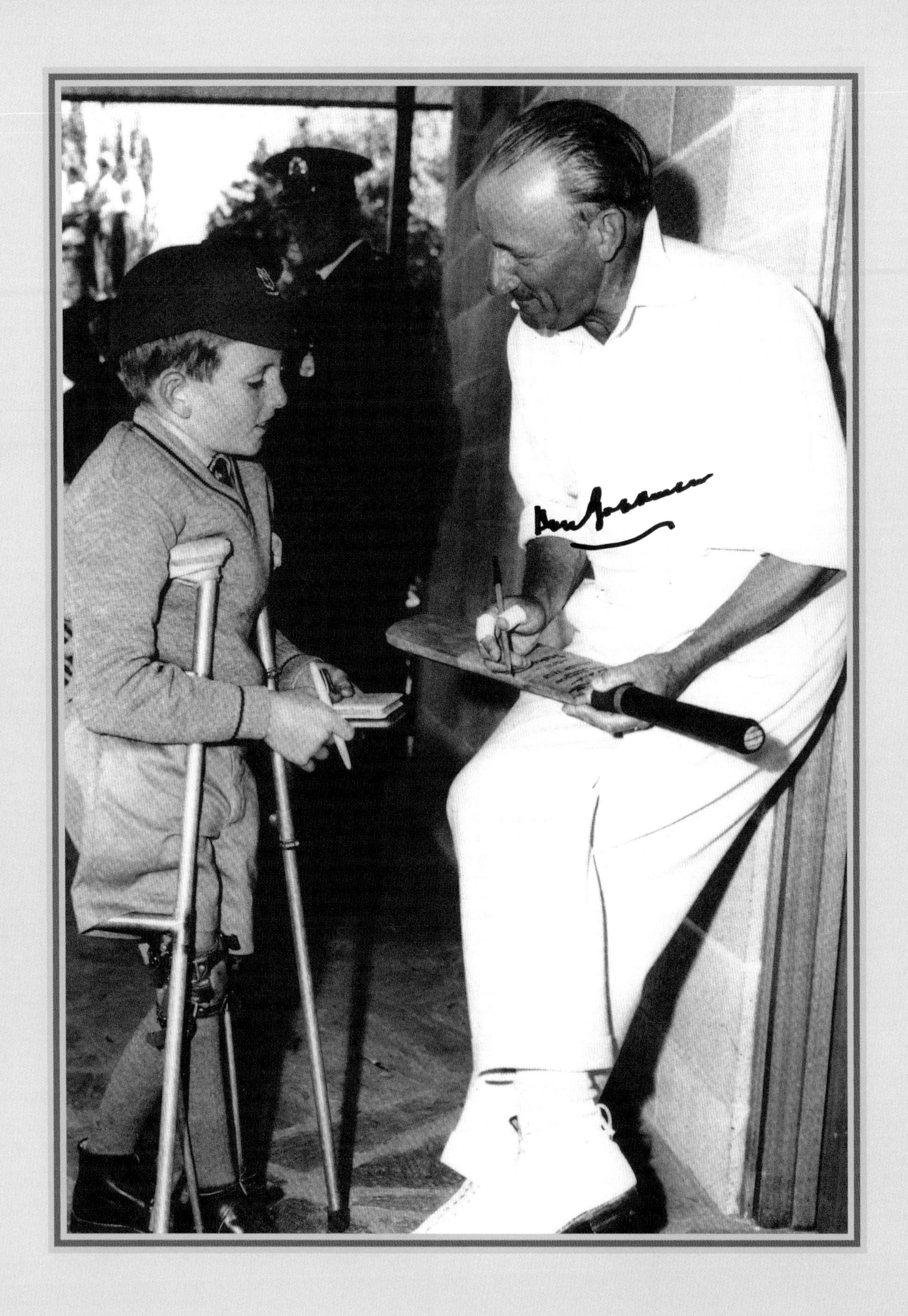

CHAPTER NINETEEN

A heart of gold & other anecdotes

Bradman wasn't the 'tough' guy many thought he was...

Bradman Invincible Bill Brown said batting with Don Bradman never lost its fascination, so purposeful was he right from the start of an innings.

'Even if he was getting along to 200 he'd still stretch you and turn a one into a two and a two into a three,' Brown said. 'You really had to scamper to keep up with him.

'The fans loved him of course and very seldom would Don let them down. He'd get a quick single off the first ball and away he'd go and take over the game.

'He wouldn't call for your runs, but you knew you had to be on your toes for his. He liked to pick up some quick singles before he got going.'

Brown insisted he wasn't 'the tough guy a lot of people think'.

'He really had a heart of gold,' he said.

'We [NSW] played against Victoria at the Sydney Cricket Ground once (in 1933-34). I needed about 30 for my 100 and the new ball was just about due. In those days it was 200 runs, not [a minimum number of] overs.

'"Bill," he said to me. "We must get your 100 before the next new ball," and proceeded to just take singles.

'I managed to get the 100 and he was just 15 or 16. It showed he really did care for his partners.

OPPOSITE, February, 1963: the Don autographs a bat for polio victim Rick Scherwin at Canberra's Manuka Oval

'By the time I was into my 120s, he'd passed me! And all in less than an hour's play. He really went for it that day.'

Brown says his job as NSW's opening bat was to take the shine off the new ball and make it easier for the batsmen to follow. 'Jack Fingleton and I would open and if we had a good day we'd bat until lunchtime. After lunch the crowd would give you twenty minutes to half an hour before getting restless because you were batting in Bradman's time.

'The word would have got around Sydney that Bradman was batting that afternoon. The crowd would double and even treble to see him.

'Not only would the bowler and fieldsmen appeal if you got hit on the pads, the whole 30,000-40,000 would appeal too! When you got out you got the most tremendous ovation, not because you played well, but because you were getting out of the way for Don!

'The grounds would swell at lunchtime, anticipating a big Bradman innings. If he happened to get out, there'd be this great exodus for the turnstiles.'

A SCARRING EXPERIENCE

When he was first selected for New South Wales for the southern tour, in 1927, Don Bradman had never been out of the state. He was a country kid, naïve in so many ways, especially to the whims of teammates who delighted in sending him into the Adelaide streets late at night on fictitious errands or having him play the piano topless so they could decide if piano playing promoted extra muscle.

Noted cricket writer Ray Robinson said the pranks scarred the sensitive young maestro and were a factor in him preferring the solitude of his own hotel room, having a quiet cup of tea and listening to classical music at night rather than spending time downstairs with rowdy teammates at the bar.

ANSWERING AN SOS

Ted Pickett thought there was a chance that he was going to lose his job because of the Don...

The multi-gifted twenty-year-old had been selected to keep wickets for Tasmania against the 1930 Australian tourists. But his employers, the Launceston *Examiner*, where he worked on the front counter, would only agree to granting him the time off if they could have a photograph of Pickett wicketkeeping while the Don, cricket's new world record-holder, was at the crease.

The Don made 22 and was out before the *Examiner's* photographer arrived. Pickett thought he'd 'be for it' and explained his predicament to Bradman at the luncheon interval. The Don agreed to go out to the centre and have his picture taken with a smiling Pickett crouched down behind the stumps.

'He wouldn't put his pads back on but I was very grateful to Don,' said Pickett, who later became Australian snooker champion. 'People couldn't understand why he was pictured at the crease without his pads. But it all turned out okay...and I kept my job!'

THE LAST LAUGH

Bill Black couldn't help boasting to his mates how he'd dismissed the record-breaker in a scratch match on the mats one day at Lithgow. Six weeks later the pair were opposed again, on the malthoid at Blackheath, Bradman being on strike when Black was introduced into the attack.

'What sort of bowler is this fellow?' Bradman asked the 'keeper', Leo Waters.

'Don't you remember this bloke?' came the reply. 'He bowled you in the exhibition match at Lithgow a few weeks ago. And he hasn't shut up about it ever since.'

Black, a fastish off-break bowler, had just two overs this time... for 62... of which the Don clobbered 60, on his way to a whirlwind 256!

A RARE WINDFALL

Australian-born Brit Arthur Whitelaw gifted the Don £1000 after his epic 334 at Leeds in 1930 'in appreciation of his wonderful performance'. The gift was almost double the £600 per player touring fee. The Don's teammates each received ash trays.

WISE AFTER THE EVENT

The Don was honeymooning in Canada and America with Arthur Mailey's team (1932) when he asked one of the local umpires, standing well to the side of the stumps, how he could possibly give an lbw. 'You wait and see,' said the umpire.

Within minutes the Don was on his way, leg before, vowing to never query an umpire again!

WONDROUS

During the tour, the Don met the great American baseballer Babe Ruth at Yankee Stadium. Writing in *The Don Meets The Babe* (1995), Bradman said: 'I had the utmost difficulty explaining cricket to him and can still hear the bewilderment in his slow American drawl as he said: "You mean to tell me you don't have to run when you hit the ball?"'

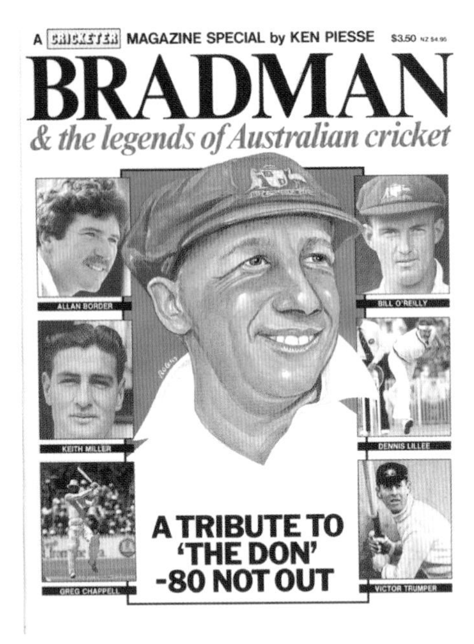

WISE WORDS

Headingley groundsman Dick Moulton had been in charge of the Test strips when Bradman made 334 in 1930 and 304 in 1934. Approaching the 1938 Test, he insisted that the Don 'wouldn't get 300 this time'. He was right. Bradman was out for 103.

A THROWAWAY LINE TO REMEMBER

The Don loved the Victorian express Ernie McCormick not only for his bowling but for his flaming sense of humour. The pair were participating in a radio interview on match-eve in Melbourne and as a throwaway line, Ernie promised that if he was bowling when Don came to the wicket the following morning he would make sure that the Don would not score from his first ball.

Bradman came in on cue, just when McCormick was bowling. The field was carefully set: six slips, mid-off, cover and extra cover. Literally no one was on the leg side. Ernie delivered the ball at pace, as he did and pitched it at least a foot outside the off stump and going away. At the last possible moment, Bradman skipped across his crease and flicked it to just inside the fence at square leg... and the batsmen ran five!

A REST IN MID-INNINGS

Bruce Bowley, a former clubmate of Bradman's at Kensington, happened to bat ahead of Bradman one day only to be told by the large crowd to make himself invisible as soon as possible: 'We didn't come to see you, mate!'

Bowley said Bradman the club batsman liked to corner the strike in the first two or three overs to allow his partner to assimilate to the conditions. 'Then as the day wore on, suddenly he'd have a period where he wouldn't have any of the strike,' he told author Margaret Geddes in *Remembering Bradman*. 'You'd have all the strike because he would be having a rest. And that I believe is one of the main reasons why he used to make so many big scores.'

PERSUASIVE DON

But for Don Bradman's intervention in 1945-46, Australia's first great left-arm paceman 'Big Bill' Johnston may never have quickened up.

Johnston had first been selected for Victoria as a slow bowler in the early years of the war, but Pearl Harbor was bombed and interstate cricket was immediately abandoned. Johnston was one of the leading wicket-takers at District first XI standard, bowling his slows, before being asked to bowl fast in the absence of anyone else.

Bradman, a Test selector, was managing South Australia's XI during an interstate match at St Kilda and was particularly impressed by Johnston's opening burst, which included wickets in each of his first two overs.

'I bowled spinners in that game as well and Don had a word to me at lunch on the final day. "I've seen you bowl, Bill," he said, "but I don't know if you spin the ball enough on first-class wickets. If you are interested in improving your game, you'd be better off organising your fast bowling and concentrating on that. There are not too many fast bowlers around at the moment, but there are quite a few spinners."

'Shortly afterwards I was down at the Old Scotch Ground one night practising with the Colts when Jack Ryder (the ex-Australian Test captain) asked me to bowl fast at him. I had no great control, but I bowled faster and at one stage I thought I almost knocked his head off. He was in his mid-50s then. Thankfully he got out of the road.

'It must have impressed him as he reckoned I should have been able to bowl eight balls an over fast rather than just one or two. I told him it was too much like hard work and I didn't want to do it. But he persisted.'

Ironically after being one of Australia's leading players on the Invincibles tour in 1948, 'Big Bill' dismissed the Don in his final two first-class innings, in Melbourne during the Don's own testimonial match, when he made his 117th and final first-class hundred and several weeks later, in Adelaide when Bradman made a farewell appearance as part of Arthur Richardson's testimonial.

During his Melbourne farewell, Johnston was bowling when Bradman, on 97, was famously dropped by Colin McCool at deep square leg, McCool kicking the ball into the fence to give Bradman a much-celebrated ton. Asked if McCool's action could possibly have been deliberate, Johnston said: 'I don't know. I never asked Col. He'd made ground to it and had to catch it over his shoulder. It landed on his toe and he (accidentally) kicked it over the boundary. It took Don to 101… There was all this cheering. It was a popular drop, I do know that.'

AN EXPERT, OF SORTS

My mother, bless her, has grown to love cricket after years of cricket talk, firstly from my father and then me. Dad was a handyman, you had to be in those days, and in-between building chores, he would sit with Mum for a cuppa and ask what the cricket score was.

One day, without being prompted, she proudly announced the score and said: 'And Bradman has just been caught in Bedser's leg trap!'

After a pause, Dad said to her: 'And Patty, what exactly is Bedser's leg trap?' She had no idea.

A DISTINGUISHED OCCASION

Eric Hollies is forever remembered as the man who bowled Bradman for a duck, with a second ball wrong-'un at the Oval in 1948.

Hollies had bowled against the Don at Edgbaston several weeks earlier and reckoned Bradman had failed to pick his googly and vowed to give him 'an early one' if he got the chance. One of the youngsters in England's team that memorable day was 21-year-old debutant John Dewes. He said the aura around the Don as he walked into bat and received three cheers from the English team was unforgettable. 'It was almost like the Prime Minister was out there,' he said.

ATTACK IS THE BEST METHOD

The Don and Australia's Prime Minister Sir Robert Menzies were the closest of friends, the Don a particular admirer of Menzies' way with words. The PM was at his loquacious best when the Don, then 54, agreed to play one last match and what's more captain Menzies' XI in a one-day friendly against the touring MCC team at Manuka Oval in the summer of 1962-63.

While the Don made only four, he led with his usual conviction,

The Don and Australia's then cricket-loving Prime Minister, Sir Robert Menzies, at Manuka Oval, 1962-63. The PM's XI played the MCC in a one-day friendly and the Don, then aged 54, made 4

as one of his team, Canberra leg-spinner and noted raconteur Graham Smith, can readily attest. He introduced Smith early and asked him where he'd like his field.

'I know this ground well, Sir Donald,' began Graham. 'If possible, I'd like to have two blokes back straight, one at long-on and one at long-off.'

'Oh no,' said the Don. 'We want to encourage them to hit them in the air, Graham. Let's play them up … for now.'

The first six balls disappeared for four, most from skiers to the unguarded long-on boundary. After the sixth, Smith approached the Don and pointing to a sprinkler hole nearby said he was thinking of jumping into it.

'Sir Donald,' said Smith, 'do you think we have encouraged them enough now?' Having agreed to an extra boundary rider, the next ball was hit straight up into the air, softening Smith's embarrassment. His opening over analysis: 0.7-0-24-1!

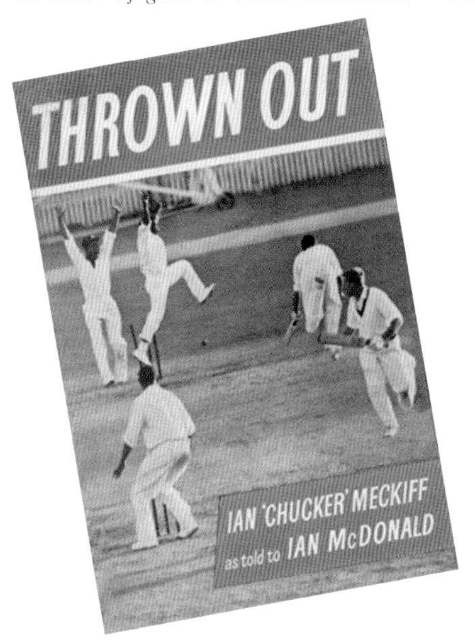

ILL LUCK

A young Ian Chappell had driven a daisy-cutter with all his power into the covers in Adelaide when the athletic New South Welshman Terry Lee dived and took a freakish catch just centimetres from the ground. Later in the rooms Chappell was still shaking his head at his ill luck, when in came the Don, smiled and said: 'It just goes to show you, Ian, what can happen when you hit the ball in the air!'

A LUCKY BREAK

Richie Benaud was once reflecting on his ill luck in never having bowled to Bradman, the Don having retired the very summer Benaud started.

'Son,' said Keith Miller, after a pause, 'that may just be the luckiest break you ever get!'

THE MECKIFF AFFAIR

As a long-time national selector, Don Bradman was one of those responsible for having exposed the suspect-actioned Victorian Ian Meckiff in 1963. Few did more to help clean up throwing than Bradman.

Ian Meckiff, cruelly no-balled out of cricket

Leading into the first South African Test, even captain Richie Benaud was surprised when Meckiff was recalled for his first Tests in almost three years. 'I didn't expect him to be in that side. And I don't think Ian expected to be in that side,' said Benaud.

'Two people on that (national) selection committee must have voted for him. Jack Ryder (the ex-Victorian) would have been one,

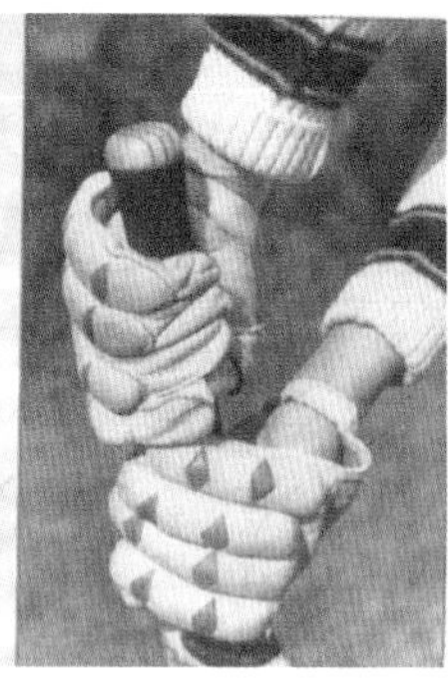

The Don's unique grip on the bat, with the left wrist turned over until it was at the back of the handle

but I was never able to find out if it was a 3-0 selection or whether it was 2-1.

'I do know that when the Lord Mayoral cocktail party was held the night before the game in Brisbane, the three selectors stayed in three of the four corners of the room. They weren't seen chatting to one another, or having a quiet drink as they normally did. I thought to myself: "There's something going on here."

'It was a very disheartening thing not just for "Mecko" but for everyone involved.'

WORDS OF WISDOM (1)

In retirement, the Don loved to spend an hour or two watching play from the South Australian committee room. He had his own favourite seat and players would always look out for him, wanting to impress. He'd go into the rooms, too, and have a cup of tea and a chat. Greg Chappell was just beginning his magnificent career and after they exchanged 'Good mornings' the Don said to him: 'And by the way, Greg, I'd change that grip if I was you.'

Bradman explained how he held the bat and how a slight variance would allow Chappell greater scope for off-side shots, without losing his exquisite touch through the leg side. 'It might be uncomfortable to start with, but give it a go,' he suggested.

Chappell said thank you and as the Don was leaving, he added: 'I've given this piece of advice to one other person and he didn't take it ... he's no longer playing.'

Chappell grabbed two bowling partners in Jeff Hammond and Terry Jenner and trialled the new grip immediately in the nets at the back of the grandstand. 'I stuck with it from then on and have no doubt it helped me enormously,' he said.

Chappell was to be the first to break the Don's long-standing record mark of 6996 Test runs.

WORDS OF WISDOM (2)

It was Bradman who first alerted the Australian selectors to the prodigious talents of David Hookes, who made five centuries in six innings in a purple patch mid-way through the season leading into the Centenary Test. He wrote to national selector Sam Loxton, imploring him to select Hookes as he was just the stroke-player cricket needed. 'Sammy, I know I'm out of line here, but I implore you. Pick Hookes for the Centenary Test.'

Loxton and Co. did as they were told and 21-year-old Hookes made a thrilling contribution to one of the games of the century.

A SURE THING

Australian cricket's mystery bowler of the '60s, John Gleeson, was known as 'The Tamworth Twister' for the unusual way he imparted each way spin with the merest flick of a finger.

Don Bradman was as fascinated as everyone else by the spinning new boy and when NSW came to Adelaide, he borrowed a bat and stood at the striker's end in his civvies, asking Gleeson to send him down some deliveries so he could personally assess the young man's abilities. Exactly 12 months later, Gleeson was promoted to the Test team.

ONELINERS (1)

In the rooms in Adelaide one day, the Don was asked how he'd go playing one-day cricket. 'I'd probably average half of what I did in Test cricket,' he said, and with a mischievous grin, added, 'but I am 80 years old you know!'

ONELINERS (2)

At a team dinner in Adelaide to mark Allan Border's first Test as captain in 1984-85, Australian opener John Dyson asked Sir Donald, a special guest, how long his bats tended to last.

'About 1000 runs a bat, John,' he said.

'So just a couple of hits then, Don!' came the instant reply.

UP CLOSE AND PERSONAL WITH THE DON

Like the Don, Billy Watson was a proud man of St George, being among the club's top all-time runmakers as well as representing Australia on its first-ever tour to the West Indies in 1955.

Billy had first seen the Don, up front and personal, as a 14-year-old when he and his cousin rode their bikes onto the old Sydney Cricket Ground No.2 and watched the Australians practice for the Ashes Test of 1946-47.

'Most people were behind the nets but being young and adventurous we cycled out onto the ground and sat down not that far back to watch. We recognised Bradman and there were a lot of press people, too, standing to the side. Don't think we should have been out there but no-one actually told us that. Next minute a drive from Keith Miller whistled past my ear. I never saw it. My cousin said it missed me by inches and Bradman marched over. He was very annoyed, no doubt because I'd nearly been hit and told us to bugger off. That was the first time we'd met.

'The next time was over in Perth very early one morning before a game against WA (in 1956-57). I was a six o'clock riser and went

Billy Watson breakfasted with the Don and went on to score a double century

down early for breakfast. We were at the old Palace hotel and it had a huge breakfast room and there was only one other bloke there when I arrived.

'I picked myself a table and sat down and no sooner had I done that but this figure walked in the same door I'd come in. It was Sir Donald. He immediately came over and made me feel so much at ease, asking if I'd had a good night's sleep and how I must be looking forward to the game.

"We talked of many subjects, just as if we'd been friends for 30 or 40 years.

"That first meeting back at the SCG had always been in the back of my mind. But after having breakfast though with the great man, my estimation of him shot up about 200 percent! I made 206 too in that game, my highest ever score.'

THE UNBEATABLES

Even some of the game's finest have been dropped, the Don included, after his first Test in 1928. For fun, we picked a team of those who had been dropped and reckon it would beat just about anyone, at any time!

In batting order:
Bill Ponsford
Bill Lawry
Don Bradman
Ricky Ponting
Steve Waugh
Michael Clarke
Keith Miller
Ian Healy
Shane Warne
Graham McKenzie
Jeff Thomson

Fun-loving Keith Miller, right, with Lindsay Hassett and Ian Craig, 1953

STORY OF A LIFETIME

Don Bradman prized his privacy and rarely gave interviews, especially later in life. It made the time the Don granted Melbourne *Herald* journalist Graham Eccles an audience even more precious. For Eccles it was like interviewing royalty...the highpoint of his career.

The Don was chairman of the Australian Cricket Board as well as a national selector and during the rain-ruined Christmas Test in

Melbourne in 1970-71 he told Eccles he simply wouldn't be interviewed. Refusing to take no for an answer, Eccles waited a few hours and phoned again, this time speaking with Jessie, Lady Bradman, who promised that Don, or she, would ring back.

Eccles had to fill his page 2 feature *On the Spot* and Bradman was his last hope for the following day's edition. He and photographer Ken Rainsbury went to Bradman's hotel and about 8.00 am the following day rang from the downstairs lobby. Bradman answered, again said no and said he didn't have anything to say anyway.

Eccles said he did, reminded him how Melbourne was his favourite city, the MCG his ultimate wicket, how he (Eccles) was up against it time-wise and how he had nothing else on stand-by to fill the space. He'd be most appreciative if he could chat…

There was a pause and then an 'Oh, all right, come up.'

He and Rainsbury hopped into the lift, knocked quietly on the door and Bradman answered saying, 'Hello Graham. Do you mind if I finish my prunes?'

'He got back on his bed, finished his breakfast and away we went. It was just the easiest interview I'd conducted in 40 years,' said Eccles. 'He was forthright and answered everything. He was great. It was so intimate I couldn't believe it. I just felt like I was a member of the family sitting on the end of the bed; it was like coming in and having a chat with your parents.'

Forty minutes later, Eccles had his story and back at the *Herald* office he was typing slip after slip, with the editor taking each one as he finished it.

'It was the biggest thing we'd done in ages,' said Eccles. 'We'd got the Don!'

CHAPTER TWENTY

Letters from the Don

They remind us of old feuds and are a fascinating insight into Australian cricket's secret history ...

The most famous cricket tour of all by Don Bradman's 'Invincibles' to England in 1948 almost went ahead without the great man. A file of 100 letters written to and from Don Bradman and now held in Sydney's Mitchell Library reveal the business pressures and health problems Australia's greatest player endured in his final playing years.

The letters enhance Bradman's reputation as a caring and visionary administrator who championed brighter cricket and silently brokered many of the law changes which still benefit the game today. They also reopened old wounds and behind-the-scenes spats with some of his greatest contemporaries and critics, including Bill 'Tiger' O'Reilly and Keith Miller. The letters came from the family of E. A. 'Chappie' Dwyer, Australia's unofficial chairman of selectors from 1930-52.

With E. A. 'Chappie' Dwyer

Dwyer was a father figure, benefactor and client of Bradman's, their friendship dating back to the late 1920s when Bradman was fast-tracked into the New South Wales XI and within eighteen months was playing for Australia. He would lend the Don his car when Bradman was in Sydney on business and wrote hundreds of

SIR DONALD BRADMAN

2 HOLDEN STREET.
KENSINGTON PARK.
SOUTH AUSTRALIA

5/2/57

Dear Chappie, I was quite appalled during my Sydney visit to find so much complacency about this game of cricket and glad to know you are seized with the gravity of its problems. I enclose a series of wonderful articles written by Jim Swanton at the end of the 1956

letters to him, discussing cricket, family, stocks and shares. The pair, along with the Victorian Jack Ryder, would select teams after a pre-booked telephone hook-up.

The Dwyer–Bradman correspondence remained in the hands of the Dwyer family until 2002.

Dwyer was distraught when Bradman told him he was simply too busy and not physically well enough to return for a fourth and final 'goodwill tour' to England in 1948. 'I do not know how to express my disappointment at your decision not to make the trip to England,' wrote Dwyer. 'But I can fully appreciate your decision and know that there is no other that you could have arrived at. I am sure everybody in the game appreciates the sacrifices you made during the last season and realise you cannot keep jeopardising your future and keep making sacrifices which are not appreciated by some people.'

Bradman's off-field feuding with ex-teammates and newspaper columnists, including Miller, O'Reilly and Jack Fingleton, occasionally spilled into the public arena without comment by the Don, who would maintain a public silence. However, in his letters to Dwyer, he shows his contempt and distaste of his critics. 'Every year that passes helps to show some of these boys up in their true colours,' he says. Australia's then Cricket Board of Control is portrayed as a virtual Old Boy's club, dominated by QCs who administered in a manner calculated to suit themselves rather than the game.

Both Bradman and Dwyer say the problems emanated from board

chairman Aubrey Oxlade, who was at the helm when the controversial Sid Barnes took on the board in 1952 in a selection squabble which landed in the Supreme Court. Bradman, a Barnes ally, along with Dwyer and the third selector, Ryder, had named Barnes in Australia's Christmas Test XII in Adelaide in 1951-52, only for the board to veto the choice on grounds other than cricket.

On a separate issue, where Bradman was using his influence to implement a law change against the use of persistent short-pitched bowling, Dwyer writes in one note: 'At discussions, the chairman of the board (Oxlade) suggested that a line be drawn across the wicket and anything short of that would be a no-ball. I am afraid it would be most imprudent for me to comment further.'

When the NSW Cricket Association led the move to alter the laws and outlaw the excessive use of bouncers — at Bradman's behest — Dwyer writes: 'I know you will smile as there is not one word in the suggestions contained in the newspaper report that emanated from the executive committee!'

Bradman also lobbied for years to have the front foot no-ball rule changed, but he lost that one.

His comments on budding Australian cricketers, including a young captain-to-be Richie Benaud, were included among the letters.

Bradman initially served as a Test selector in 1936-37 when he first led his country. His last selection duties were in 1970-71 when he and fellow selectors Neil Harvey and Sam Loxton named expressman Dennis Lillee virtually sight unseen. This panel was also responsible for the mid-series sacking of Bill Lawry as captain, Lawry learning of his fate via a radio report.

His massive involvement in cricket administration officially ended in June 1986.

Excerpts from the Don's letters to 'Chappie' Dwyer:

1 January 1938: 'After having been absolutely roasted here [in Melbourne] on Saturday I am nearly freezing this morning. Not even C. B. Fry's wardrobe would be able to cope with this place…'

25 January 1946: 'An Australian XI without a slow leg break bowler would be lost.'

6 February 1946: 'For the sixth batsman (to New Zealand), I don't care whether you pick (Bill) Alley, (Ken) Meuleman or (Des) Fothergill. On what I have seen, Meuleman looks the best and has

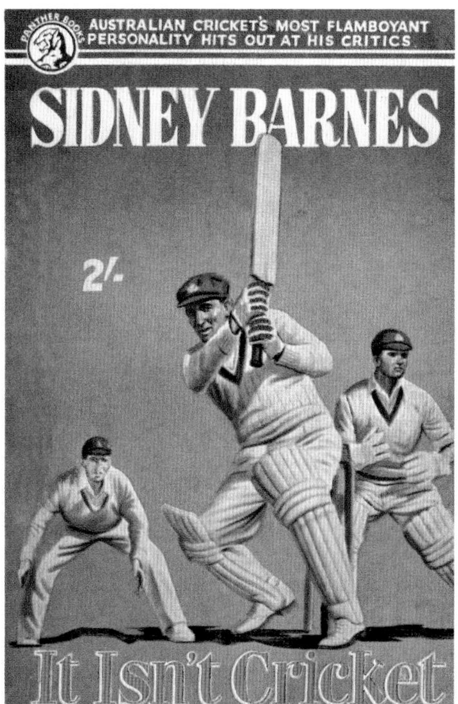

the brightest future. On the other hand Jack (Ryder) seems to have preference for Fothergill whereas Alley's record is exceptionally good and he is a left-hander.'

20 March 1946: 'Newcomer (Merv) Harvey produced the finest innings I've seen for the season. His batting was magnificent, almost flawless. And despite the weakness of the attack, he appealed to me as a player of Test calibre. Watch him closely next year.'

23 August 1946: 'Now that O'Reilly appears to be out of the Test matches we may have to use Tribe and as he is such an unusual type, I don't think we should give the Englishmen any more opportunities of seeing him than are necessary (vetoing George Tribe's selection for the MCC-Australian XI match at the start of the 1946-47 tour).'

23 October 1946: 'I don't think (Ron) Saggers is a good keeper. I also think his batting is overrated. I strongly oppose his selection and think we should undoubtedly give Ben (Barnett) this opportunity. To define our ideas (for the coming Australian XI game), I would put this to you, that one opening batsman for the Test matches must be Brown, but his partner is not yet definite. The next four batsmen subject to my being available must be Bradman, (Sid) Barnes, (Lindsay) Hassett and (Keith) Miller.

'This question of selecting a team by phone is rather unsatisfactory but it can't be helped...'

(And a postscript): 'Have just seen (Bruce) Dooland and asked him re. West Australian players and he wasn't very impressed. Says (Ken) Cumming and (Charlie) Puckett not as fast as W. (Bill) Johnston but pretty accurate — former purely in-swinger. (David) Watt somewhat crude and doubts if solid enough for the big stuff.'

17 March 1947: 'Had I seen (Bill) O'Reilly's niggardly description of the last day of the fifth Test before I wrote my eulogy of him, I may have omitted my reference to his mental ability. Do these fellows get any pleasure out of harbouring jealousy?'

March 1947: 'The textile business calls me to England next year... cricket seems out of the question. I know you cherish the hope that I'll play but I don't see any possibility at all of reconsidering it.'

15 May 1947: 'England without (Doug) Wright would be only half a side.'

1 July 1947: 'I've had very tempting (UK) press offers, but am very dubious about going at all under present day conditions (and business pressures). Might be better in 1952.'

HOTEL WINDSOR

Monday

Dear Chappie

After having been absolutely roasted here on Saturday I am nearly freezing this morning. Not even CB Fry's wardrobe would be able to cope with this place.

You were kind enough to suggest that you might be

3 May 1948: 'It was only what I expected of (Jack) Fingleton and I feel you can understand that he will not receive any further privileges on the tour as far as I am concerned...

'It is a little too early to give you any idea as to how the boys will shape up in the big matches. I can only say as far as the batting of the new players (is concerned that it) has been somewhat disappointing because of their lack of adaptability to the slower, turning wickets, however experience may remedy that. On the other hand the boys are pulling together remarkably well — it is not going too far to say that up to this stage they are the happiest team with which I have travelled — here's hoping it continues...

'Please do not expect letters from me on tour because apart from the normal duties when I tell you that I got 500 letters in the first two days of this week you will have some idea of what the correspondence is like.'

15 November 1948: 'The boys really moulded into a great side in the finish and I think if you speak to any of them they will support me in my view that it would have taken an exceptional team to have beaten us with normal luck.

'I felt very happy personally to think that I got through so well, although not without many anxious moments (with rib cartilage problems) and I would like to have a good rest even now to recuperate.'

18 April 1950: 'The only adverse comment I can make at the moment is that you apparently ruined Langley's physique (when Dwyer managed the 1949-50 Australian team to South Africa), because surely he will never play football until he takes off two stone.'

20 February 1951: 'I have been putting up with such personal insults for years. What about the experience when I first captained Australia (in 1936-37)? I just had to take it on the chin and be blamed for close associates even for the Board's action in putting players on the mat when I was not only innocent but completely ignorant of what was happening?' (Speaking of the between-the-wars 'sectarianism' row involving Bill O'Reilly.)

11 October 1951: 'There is a problem which I think should be clear in our minds beforehand and that is what we are going to do about (Sid) Barnes? I see that you have selected him for NSW and therefore his name must go up for discussion by the Australian selectors. The question is whether we are to select him providing we think he is good enough to be included in the team. If we do this it rests with the Board to say whether they approve of his selection or not and should the Board refuse then it would place the selection committee in a very embarrassing position if they were publicly accused of not selecting a man when in actual fact that was not the case. The question is whether in those circumstances any action should be taken to indicate to the public the true position… it may be that you would consider the question of discussing the position confidentially with the chairman of the Board…'

22 October 1951: 'It would appear that we may discard thoughts of Iverson for the first Test match because he will not be fit (he eventually played). On the other hand I am very anxious to hear your views in regard to Barnes, both as to ability and fitness. With reference to your views concerning his selection (i.e. if he is selected), I agree with you that no selection committee should be expected to bear criticism or embarrassment which would not be rightly leveled (sic) at such selection committee…I note that you have booked the phone call for 8 p.m. Sydney time on Friday and I shall of course make a point of being available.'

Early February 1952: (Opposing the consistent use of bouncers by NSW trio Ray Lindwall, Keith Miller and Alan Walker): 'This feature of our cricket constantly perturbs me but I'm not sure if you are aware of the very anti-NSW feeling that exists because of the way your fellows, without fear of retaliation, hand it out every year to visiting teams in Sydney.'

9 February 1952: 'I shall be very surprised if he [Barnes] goes any further and takes any action.'

11 February 1952: 'Jack (Ryder) would never refuse to support a Victorian for any position…(Jim) Burke is better than either (the two Victorian openers Colin McDonald and George Thoms). If he is to gain a permanent place in the Australian XI, I think that (a) he must be a regular opener for NSW with Morris, which means (Jack) Moroney going lower down if he is picked and (b) he must learn to be more aggressive. You cannot expect Jack to support Burke as an opening batsman if he is not regularly opening and it is a powerful thing to have two successful regular openers in one State.

'I agree with you about (Graeme) Hole and if your memory is good you will recall that I have expressed exactly the same opinion from the very first day I saw him, even when you were more optimistic about his future than I.

'Strangely enough you got the wrong impression about my views on (Jim) DeCourcy. I am not opposed to DeCourcy. I think he is a splendid player and better than (Graeme) Hole probably, but I thought he was much older. I shall promise to watch him closely next season.

'I do not think (Richie) Benaud will be a great bat or bowler, but he is a good cricketer. I am not impressed by your argument that he has been out so many times this year to wonderful catches. The point is that great players do not make the shots which will give those catches. However I am favourably impressed with many things about the boy and was pleased to support him for the last match and hope he gets a fair go next year.'

Late February 1952: 'I see O'Reilly joined (Clarrie) Grimmett in saying the selectors should be sacked. Surely if he is an official of your (NSW) association, he should not be allowed to write such criticism. The players are debarred from writing so why should officials be free? You ought to have a try and put this fellow in his box.'

5 March 1952: 'These NSW bowlers have also exploited the bumper when playing for Australia against other countries. In my view they have caused much feeling both in the State and the International matches. This feeling is bitter and widespread.

'Re. Barnes (and his impending Supreme Court action): My advice is for you to keep quiet as an oyster and under no circumstances say anything. I can't tell you all the moves but I'm sure that is sound. You may be forced to speak later. If so please consult me beforehand.

DON BRADMAN & CO.
Stock and Share Brokers
SIR DONALD BRADMAN
MEMBER THE STOCK EXCHANGE
OF ADELAIDE LTD.

TELEPHONE CENTRAL 822

TELEGRAPHIC ADDRESS:
"BRADMANCO" ADELAIDE

The position is very delicate. I shall await further news with interest.'
Early March 1952: (On outspoken critic and ex-teammate R. S. 'Dick' Whitington): 'Why they pay him I don't know…when he played the game he neither liked them (bumpers) or had the ability to play them…every year that passes helps to show some of these boys up in their true colors.'
Mid March 1952: 'It would be unfair to expect other States to take the lead by protesting against the State which possesses all the fast bowlers. On the other hand if the latter State (NSW) signifies its willingness to take action, it would create much goodwill amongst those States who at present are bitter against NSW.

'I would remind you that the day will certainly come when other States will be well supplied with fast bowlers and NSW will have none and if this thing is not stopped, it will be the NSW batsmen who will be getting belted in years to come. It is a bad thing for Australian cricket and cricket in general and we ought to do something about it now so that it is cleared up before this team goes to England. If it is not, I can see trouble ahead because there will be no restraining hand at the top.'
28 April 1952: 'One of the great troubles of the Board at present is that things are discussed far too much from the legal angle instead of the common sense and practical angle. What we badly need are a few men with practical playing experience so that when we discuss a vital matter so affecting cricket, such as for instance this bumper business, the delegates will understand the importance of what they are talking about.'
22 May 1953: 'They (Lindsay Hassett's Ashes tourists) are doing better that I anticipated.'
21 December 1953: 'I am not sure that I shall stay there [on the board] but more of that I shall not put in a letter'.
16 February 1956: 'Quite a good Board meeting. The chairman behaved himself and the new member S. W. (Syd Webb) got a taste of red tape which I fear irked him somewhat.'
Mid-March 1956: 'There is a tremendous cricket program coming up for the next eight years and during that time much good or harm can be done.'
17 October 1956: (In a postscript)…'meanwhile Chappie keep your eyes out for some good cricketers'.
Late October 1956: 'You seem to be taking Miller's insinuations more calmly than most and I am not sure we should regard his utter-

ances as unimportant. He has accused me of a breach of confidence in my official capacity as a selector. That is a lie, too and I am still a selector. I feel I have the right to take the matter very seriously. Apparently you don't look at it my way but I think you would if you were still a selector.

'I am not sure what action I shall take but don't you think in fairness to ourselves and to Jack Ryder we should acquaint the board that we are not guilty of Miller's charges?' (And, in a postscript): 'Boys are doing better in India without KRM (Miller)'.

5 February 1957: 'The whole history and evolution of cricket is change. Practically nothing remains as it was. The size and shape of all implements have been altered, all measurements have been changed except for the length of the pitch, the method of bowling, follow-on, (use of) the new ball etc and as for lbws...nine revisions were made in a less than (a) 60 year period.

'(Yet) I am accused of wanting to tinker with the laws as though I'm a criminal. I want to see people hitting the ball to bring the public through the turnstiles.'

Mid February 1957: 'I am absolutely thrilled at the proposal (from the Marylebone CC) to restrict the on-side field. I don't mind so much about the five altogether. It is two only behind the wicket which is the kernel of it all.

'We will get this game right eventually despite some of the numb skulls...If you can't get your (NSW) association to support MCC, I'm a Dutchman.'

12 April 1957: 'I am appalled that the NSWCA is so pigheaded over this thing. However, I have no doubt that if the MCC requests us to try the experiment they will agree. Some of your friends would refuse to try anything DGB suggested, but if Lord Thingumme suggested it — even though he knew nothing about cricket — they would agree like a shot. Funny isn't it...

'I am optimistic that we can see daylight ahead but we must be prepared to persevere and work — not be discouraged by temporary setbacks by the old no-hopers. It is the good of cricket for which we must work. Indeed it is more than that — it may even be the survival for without public support the game will die.'

CHAPTER TWENTY-ONE

The Midas touch

Don Bradman was directly responsible for twelve Australian victories during his 52-match reign as the game's outstanding batsman ...

MARCH 1929, FIFTH TEST V ENGLAND, MELBOURNE

In a contest which stretched to eight days — all Tests in Australia being of a 'timeless' nature in those days — Don Bradman was crucial in Australia's only win of a one-sided rubber.

In his first series and just his fourth appearance, Bradman made 123 and 37 not out. It was the young maestro's second century in as many MCG Tests. The win was greeted joyfully as Australia had lost each of the first four Tests and in the fifth had to chase an English first innings total of 500-plus.

In the first innings, while Sydney debutant Alan Fairfax defended, young Bradman attacked, rattling to his first 50 in just 71 minutes before completing his second Test hundred in 172 minutes. Their stand was worth 183. Australia's first innings of 491 consumed a marathon 271 eight-ball overs.

In the second innings after Adelaide paceman Tim Wall had taken 5-66 to restrict England's lead, 20-year-old Bradman and his 39-year-old captain Jack Ryder added an unbroken 83 to guide Australia home. Dropped after his first Test earlier in the series, Bradman's place was never again in question.

SCOREBOARD: England 519 (J. B. Hobbs 142, M. Leyland 137) and 257 (T. W. Wall 5-66) lost to Australia 491 (D. G. Bradman

OPPOSITE: with Bill Ponsford, Headingley, 1934

123, W. M. Woodfull 102, G. Geary 5-105) and 5-287 (D. G. Bradman 37 not out) by five wickets. Bradman Test No.4

JUNE 1930, SECOND TEST V ENGLAND, LORD'S

Bradman's wonderful innings of 254 was pivotal to a match Ashes devotees consider one of the most entertaining of all time. Played in superb weather at the game's headquarters, it was a game that had everything including the-then highest ever Australian Test score and the highest individual Test score at Lord's. Both records would stand for more than 60 years.

'The advent of Bradman was like combustible stuff thrown on fires of batsmanship that had been slumbering potentially. The bat sent out cracking noises; they were noises quite contemptuous,' was Sir Neville Cardus' assessment of the initial phase of the innings Bradman rated as the finest of his life. He gave not even one half-chance.

Chasing 425 and coming in after Ponsford and Woodfull had opened with 162, Bradman danced down the wicket and drove his first ball from left-arm spinner Jack 'Farmer' White for four. The stroke set the trend for the remainder of the day.

By stumps he had made 155 at better than a run a minute, without even one shot out of place. On the cloudless Monday, he added a further 99 before marginally lifting the ball for the first time to be brilliantly caught at short cover by Percy Chapman.

Despite centuries by Chapman and in the first innings Kumar Shri Duleepsinhji, Australia had only 72 to score in the second innings to win. Bradman missed out this time but the target was achieved with little drama.

SCOREBOARD: England 425 (K. S. Duleepsinhji 173) and 375 (A. P. F. Chapman 121, C. V. Grimmett 6-167) lost to Australia 6-729 dec (D. G. Bradman 254, W. M. Woodfull 155) and 3-72 by seven wickets. Bradman Test No.6

DECEMBER 1931, THIRD TEST V SOUTH AFRICA, MELBOURNE

Enjoying a phenomenal summer of success where he amassed 806 runs at an average of 200-plus, Bradman teamed up again with his captain Bill Woodfull to bat the South Africans out of the match.

Bradman's 167 was his fifth century in as many Tests on what was to become his most prolific Australian ground. With Australia facing a first innings deficit of 160, Bradman added 274 with Woodfull, then also a record for the Australian second wicket.

The South African attack, led by big swing bowler A. J. 'Sandy' Bell, had removed Australia for 198 on the first day, before Australia revived in mid-match, Bradman again pivotal. He reached his 50 in 64 minutes after tea on the third day, went to stumps on 97 and hit the first ball of day four for three to complete his 100 in 98 minutes, his fastest ever Test century. The Springboks lost by 169, the closest margin in a series they lost 5-0.

SCOREBOARD: Australia 198 (A. J. Bell 5-69) and 554 (D. G. Bradman 167, W. M. Woodfull 161) defeated South Africa 358 (K.G. Viljoen 111) and 225 (C. V. Grimmett 6-67) by 169 runs. Bradman Test No.17

JANUARY 1932, FOURTH TEST V SOUTH AFRICA, ADELAIDE

Bradman maintained his appetite and liking for the South African attack and three weeks after his 167 at the MCG he made an Australian-high 299 not out in the ten-wicket thrashing of the tourists. It was a score which remained the best in a Test down under until 1966 when Bob Cowper scored 307 in an Ashes Test in Melbourne.

The Don came to the wicket after Bill Ponsford was bowled with the total on nine and continued until the end of the innings when Brisbane debutant Hugh 'Pud' Thurlow, in at No.11, was run out as Bradman called for an unlikely second to try to complete his 300th run. Earlier Alan Kippax had been run-out without facing a ball when Bradman scampered for his 100th run.

Resuming on the third day on 170, Bradman was scratchy early, before playing with his old fluency. He had by then made centuries at all of Australia's Test venues. He continued to show an overwhelming mastery over the South Africans, with Bell the only one to restrict his scoring rate. Master spinner Clarrie Grimmett took fourteen wickets for the game.

SCOREBOARD: South Africa 308 (C. V. Grimmett 7-116) and 274 (C. V. Grimmett 7-83) lost to Australia 513 (D. G. Bradman 299 not out, A. J. Bell 5-142) and 0-73 by ten wickets. Bradman Test No.18

OPPOSITE, BOTTOM: with Archie Jackson during their fourth wicket 243-run partnership against England at The Oval in 1930. Bradman made 232 and Jackson 73

Two of Australia's other between-the-wars cricket stars: Clarrie Grimmett, opposite, top, and above, Alan Kippax

BELOW: a 1930s chart of the Don's wonderful 254

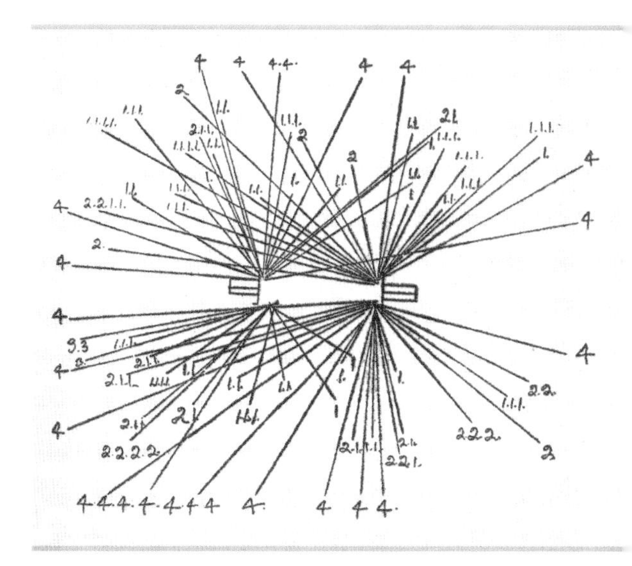

DECEMBER 1932, SECOND TEST V ENGLAND, MELBOURNE

This was most probably the most remembered match of the Don's career. His century, alongside Bill O'Reilly's ten wicket haul, was critical in Australia's only win of an acrimonious summer. England had launched its bodyline tactics in Sydney and after being soundly beaten, Australia hit back, against the odds, to draw level at 1-1, Bradman's unbeaten 103 in the second innings the cornerstone of the win.

It was a remarkable individual performance after the most famous duck of his life, first-ball, on the first morning. Having missed the first Test through illness, the Don was cheered to the wicket by an enormous crowd before dragging his first ball, a bouncer from Bill Bowes, down onto his leg stump. He walked back to stunned silence and in the rooms while unbuckling his pads turned to teammate Leo O'Brien and said: 'Fancy doing that!'

In the second innings, he opened his scoring with a hook for

December, 1932, MCG: the moment that stunned a nation - the Don bowled first ball by Bill Bowes. 'Fancy doing that,' the Don said in the dressing-room immediately afterwards

four off Bowes and motored to a century in just three hours. He sometimes faced the 'Notts Express' Harold Larwood without even one fielder on the off side. Historian David Frith said it was a knock which 'sustained the nation's fervent faith in him'.

Tiger O'Reilly's bouncing wrist spin capitalised on Bradman's effort.

SCOREBOARD: Australia 228 and 191 (D. G. Bradman 103 not out) defeated England 169 (W. J. O'Reilly 5-63) and 139 (W. J. O'Reilly 5-66) by 111 runs. Bradman Test No.20

AUGUST 1934, FIFTH TEST V ENGLAND, THE OVAL

After a modest beginning to his second English tour, Bradman finished the Test summer in a blaze of sensational scoring. He and fellow record-breaker Bill Ponsford warmed up with a 388-run stand in the fourth Test at Leeds before the Don was sidelined for six weeks with injury and illness.

He was well enough, however, to return for the fifth and final Test at The Oval and again flanked by Ponsford, added a world record 451, of which he made 244.

Despite his enforced lay-off, in which he hardly held a bat, Bradman struck the ball beautifully and in 316 minutes hit 32 fours and one six. Veteran English opener Herbert Sutcliffe, playing in his last Test, chased a shot to the boundary ropes, leant over the fence and asked: 'Anyone got any suggestions?'

'Bradman was flawless,' Sir Neville Cardus was to write of this innings. 'He gave no sign that in his extensive machine there was any seat of error.'

Having scored more than 700, Australia led by 374 runs on the first innings, but in this 'timeless' Test, Bill Woodfull did not enforce the follow-on. A second innings allowed Bradman a further 77. Eventually Clarrie Grimmett and Bill O'Reilly wrapped up victory by 562 runs and Australia had won the Ashes for the second time in fours years on 22 August, captain Woodfull's birthday. Bradman's celebrations were brief as he was soon to undergo emergency surgery for acute appendicitis.

SCOREBOARD: Australia 701 (W. H. Ponsford 266, D. G. Bradman 244) and 327 (W. E. Bowes 5-55, E. W. Clark 5-98) defeated England 321 (M. Leyland 110) and 145 (C. V. Grimmett 5-64) by 562 runs. Bradman Test No.28

JANUARY 1937, THIRD TEST V ENGLAND, MELBOURNE

Two down in the five-match rubber, Bradman was an irresistible force in turning the series around in his maiden summer as captain.

There were suggestions that some members of the team were unhappy with his leadership and several were called to front the Board of Control in Melbourne.

Only the run-ups were covered once games started and the Australians had by far the worst of the weather in the opening two Tests, being thrashed in Brisbane and Sydney. It was a nightmarish start to Bradman's captaincy.

In front of huge Melbourne crowds, Bradman failed in the Australian first innings as Australians slipped to a precarious 6-130. But this time the Englishmen were forced to bat on a rain-affected wicket. They declared nine down before a reshuffled batting order allowed Bradman and Jack Fingleton to bat in the best conditions of the match and add 346 for the sixth wicket, the crucial partnership of the summer. Bradman's innings of 270 lasted 458 minutes and contained 22 boundaries and 110 singles.

More than 350,000 people attended the six-day Test. When Bradman reached his double ton, Bradman biographer Michael Page said 'the cheering was so prolonged it held up play'.

England lost the match by a huge margin and the following two Tests as well; Australia retained the Ashes 3-2.

SCOREBOARD: Australia 9-200 dec and 564 (D. G. Bradman 270, J. H. W. Fingleton 136) defeated England 9-76 dec (M. W. Seivers 5-21) and 323 (M. Leyland 111 not out, L. O'B. Fleetwood-Smith 5-124) by 365 runs. BradmanTest No.31

MEDITERRANEAN AIR LINER CRASHES—Page 3

Greatest Sale In Victoria—Over 200,000 Daily

The Sun NEWS-PICTORIAL

Melbourne: Thursday, January 2, 1936

Bradman On The Job Again With 229 Not Out

JANUARY 1937, FOURTH TEST V ENGLAND, ADELAIDE

For the second time in back-to-back Tests, Bradman was the catalyst of an Australian victory. Australia had trailed on the first innings before the Bradman-led revival, every bit as impressive as in Melbourne in the New Year.

With Australia's batting affected by having to bat on wet wickets in two Tests and England also disadvantaged by rain in two, Bradman said that he felt this innings and this Test decided the rightful winners of the rubber.

His second innings in Adelaide was a restrained seven-hour

effort full of stern concentration. He hit just fourteen boundaries, two of them from consecutive Walter Robins deliveries which raised his century. Ninety-nine of his runs came in singles.

'The main point behind his cricket was the generalship; behind it all he was playing for Australia, not for Bradman,' said Sir Neville Cardus. This chanceless knock was Bradman's slowest ever double century. It was also his first in an Australian Ashes Test away from the MCG. Bradman's 17th Test century temporarily put him No.1 on the all-time list.

SCOREBOARD: Australia 288 and 433 (D. G. Bradman 212, W. R.

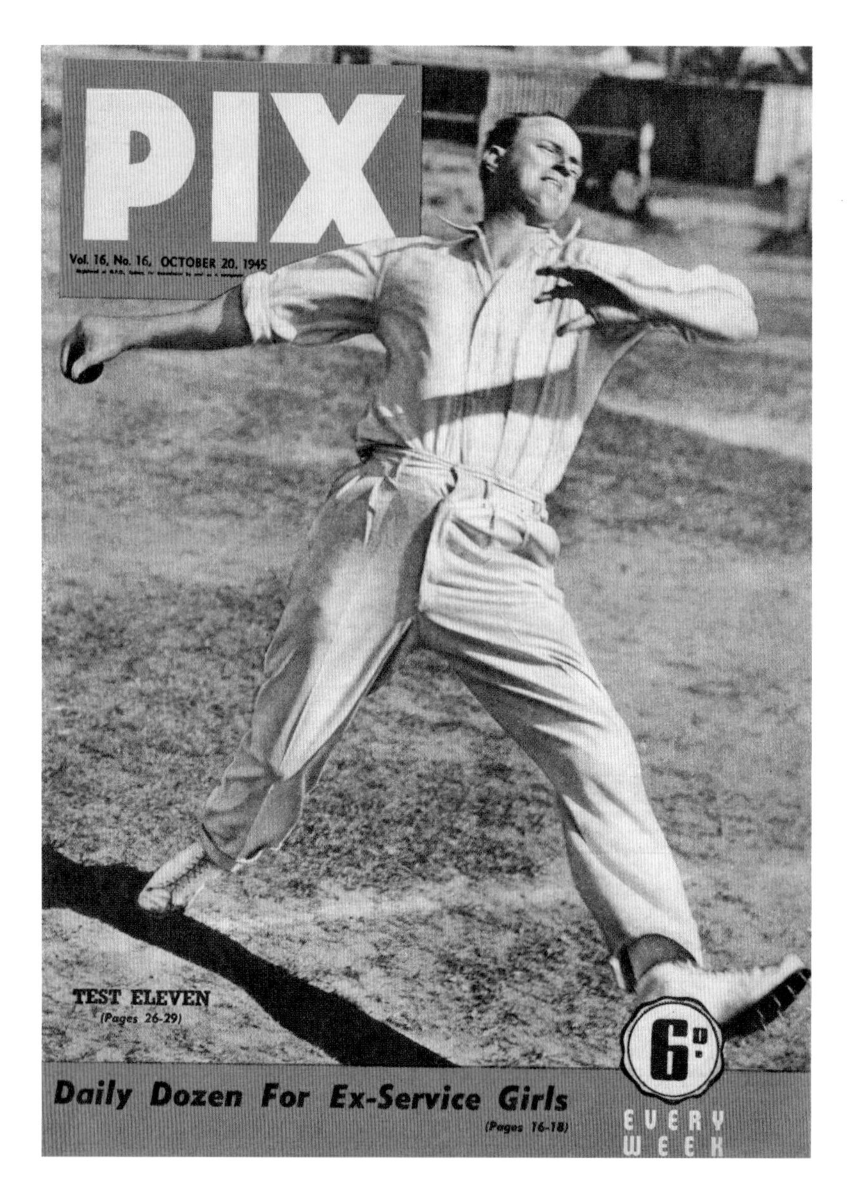

Hammond 5-57) defeated England 330 (C. J. Barnett 129) and 243 (L. O'B Fleetwood-Smith 6-110) by 148 runs. Bradman Test No.32

JULY 1938, THIRD TEST V ENGLAND, HEADINGLEY

This was a low-scoring match, ironically Bradman's 'worst ever' Test at Leeds, but one which included one of his most important innings.

On a dicey pitch Bradman's chanceless first innings of 103 set up Australia's only win in that rain-shortened four-match series. It proved just enough to hold on to those precious Ashes.

In three hours he struck just nine fours, but he was the only batsman to master Doug Wright's fast leg-breaks on the damp, turning surface in bad light. Bradman, cap-less, batted on through the dark. He was less worried by that than the prospect of having to bat on the same wicket after the rain that looked certain to fall.

'Bradman was in such form that he could have played by candle-light,' said English batting icon Jack Hobbs.

The forecast rain stayed away and the Australians led by nineteen on the first innings. Bill O'Reilly, left, was at his menacing best and helped the Australians to a five-wicket win. During this match Bradman completed his sixth century in as many Tests and passed the 5000 run mark in Tests.

SCORECARD: England 223 (W. J. O'Reilly 5-66) and 123 (W. J. O'Reilly 5-56) lost to Australia 242 (D. G. Bradman 103) and 5-107 by five wickets. Bradman Test No.36

JANUARY 1948, THIRD TEST V INDIA, MELBOURNE

Almost inevitably Bradman reserved his only twin-centuries feat in Test cricket for Melburnians. The two tons were compiled against first-time tourists India, which conceded almost as many runs as had the starstruck South Africans sixteen years previously.

Then aged 39, Bradman was 99 on the first day and completed his hundred straight after. He remained chanceless until an attack of cramp broke his concentration.

India, like England in 1936-37, fell foul of Melbourne's unreliable weather and was forced to bat on a rain-affected wicket. They tried to manoeuvre the Australians back on it before it recovered, but again Bradman adjusted his batting order and then added an unbeaten 223 with Arthur Morris for the fourth wicket. Bradman accelerated to his century in just over two hours, one writer commenting: 'He drove, pulled and hooked with the abandon of youth at picnic cricket...(it was) a glorious knock.'

Then to make the difficult become the impossible for the Indians, it rained again. They were beaten by 233.

SCOREBOARD: Australia 394 (D. G. Bradman 132) and 4-255 dec (D. G. Bradman 127 not out, A. R . Morris 100 not out) defeated India 9-291 dec (V. M. H. Mankad 116) and 125 by 233 runs. Bradman Test No.45

JUNE 1948, FIRST TEST V ENGLAND, NOTTINGHAM

Arch Bradman critic Jack Fingleton said that this century was

Bradman's most colourless. It still took only three and half hours, however, and set up the first Test win as his Invincibles continued their triumphant, unbeaten march.

More sympathetic was the BBC's John Arlott who thought that, 'Once he had played himself in, there was never any doubt that Bradman would make a century.'

In bad light, England had been bowled out for 165 on the first day and Bradman and Lindsay Hassett scored centuries as Australia built a huge lead of 344. Bradman was then caught in a leg trap off a big inswinger from the lion-hearted Alec Bedser. He fell in identical fashion in his next two innings, including a duck in the second

August, 1948: Neil Harvey, then a teenager, made 112 on his Ashes debut

innings of this Test, prompting much forensic examination of the 40-year-old's technique.

'I refused to be tied down by an obvious plan and paid the penalty with my eyes wide open,' said Bradman.

Neither that glitch nor a big 100 from England's folk-hero Denis Compton failed to halt Australia's advance towards a comfortable victory in this Trent Bridge Test, or the next at Lord's.

SCOREBOARD: England 165 (W. A. Johnston 5-36) and 441(D. C. S. Compton 184) lost to Australia 509 (D. G. Bradman 138, A. L. Hassett 137) and 2-98 by eight wickets. Bradman Test No.48

July, 1948: Arthur Morris made 182 while sharing a match-winning triple-century stand with the Don

JULY 1948, FOURTH TEST V ENGLAND, LEEDS

Bradman saved probably his greatest triumph for his penultimate Test. Against all odds, he and Morris shared a huge partnership to allow Australia for the first time to chase down a fourth innings target of more than 400 on what was a sixth-day pitch, given Test cricket in those days was Sunday-free.

After some high scoring by both sides over the first four days, England captain Norman Yardley batted on for two overs on the final morning before setting Australia 404 to win on a broken and deteriorating pitch. Bradman said he wanted to win, but in particular, didn't want to lose. Then he was presented with an opportunity. The wicket was turning and some balls kicked, but England dropped chances, wicketkeeper Godfrey Evans had a rare shocker, and spinners Jim Laker and part-timer Compton cracked under pressure, bowling a succession of full tosses and long hops. In just 30 minutes before lunch, Australia added 64. Bradman sensed something special could be achieved.

Despite attacks of cramp, Bradman played superbly and with Morris added 301 for the second wicket in 217 exhilarating minutes. Bradman's 173 not out contained 29 fours and gave him an unsurpassed average of 192 at Leeds.

Ashes debutant Neil Harvey hit the winning boundary with twelve minutes to spare. The match was attended by 158,000 people, all of whom must have walked away marvelling once again at the sheer genius of Australia's 'Wizard of the Willow'.

SCOREBOARD: England 496 (C. Washbrook 143, W. J. Edrich 111) and 8-365 dec lost to Australia 458 (R. N. Harvey 112) and 3-404 (A. R. Morris 182, D. G. Bradman 173 not out) by seven wickets. BradmanTest No.51

DON BRADMAN

and

PETERS

ICE CREAM

CHAPTER TWENTY-TWO

Ahead of his years

Don Bradman was the first true Australian cricket celebrity and the first to truly 'cash in' on his fame...

During the '30s as Don Bradman's fame spread and 'cricket fever' raged like never before, the Don's name became synonymous with select companies and products, from boots and bats to trousers, ice-cream and even pharmaceutical products.

For his first five record-breaking years, before his transfer to Adelaide, he was full-time cricket, and when he wasn't playing, practising, or on tour, he was selling Don Bradman Complete Cricket Sets for F. J. Palmer's, doing broadcasting spots on Sydney radio station 2UE and writing feature stories for the Sydney *Sun*. He endorsed Sykes cricket bats and Don Bradman cricket boots. He even agreed to have his image used in promoting Losec medication cream, used for the treatment of ulcer conditions.

It seemed that all of Australia was Bradman-mad and advertisers queued to win his approval. His celebrity status created jealousies and dissention among at least some of the underlings, but even they could not deny his appeal.

Certainly the various state administrations loved having him in

Mr. DON BRADMAN, enjoying perfect reception with his McMichael Suitcase Portable.
The name McMichael for
the last fourteen years has stood for the highest class of radio instruments and for absolute reliability in their construction—reliability based upon a unique experience of radio reception under difficult conditions. McMichael make sets of all types to suit every requirement. This year again there is a complete range of instruments for those who appreciate radio they can *depend* upon.
McMICHAEL RADIO
McMICHAEL RADIO LTD., SLOUGH, BUCKS.

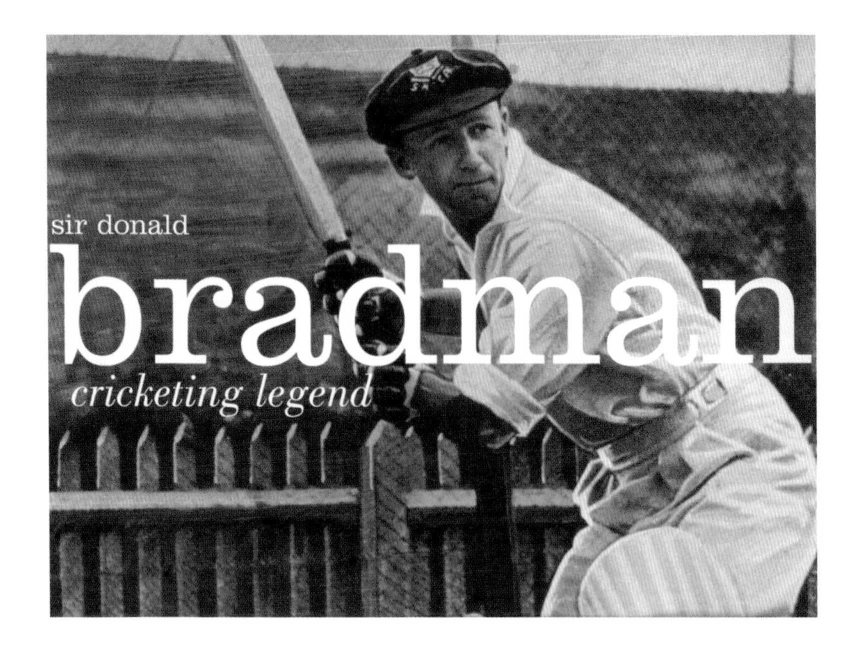
sir donald
bradman
cricketing legend

The Australian Test Team—Back Row: C. L. Badcock, W. A. Brown, J. H. Fingleton, E. L. McCormick, W. J. O'Reilly, Mr. W. H. Jeanes (Manager
E. White, L. Fleetwood-Smith, F. A. Ward, C. L. Walker. Front Row: A. L. Hassett, A. G. Chipperfield, S. J. McCabe (Vice-Captain
D. G. Bradman (Captain), B. A. Barnett, S. Barnes, M. G. Waite.
LAUREL The all-purpose kerosene WINS EVERY TES
For Lighting, Cooking, Heating, Cleaning, Freezing and Incubati

What Don Bradman did NOT Say!

LIQUOR TRADE IMPUDENCE!

IS THERE ANY LIMIT TO IT?

When Don Bradman was hitting up his century score in the Adelaide Test Match, stumps were drawn with the champion's score, "N.O., 166"!

Next morning, from one of the **"B"** Class Wireless Stations, over the air buzzed out this priceless bit of liquor-trade effrontery:

Announcer: "What did Bradman say as amidst the plaudits of the crowd he walked off the field after making **166**, not out?"

Second Announcer: "I don't know! What **did** he say?"

Answer: "I'm thirsty! Go and order two dozen of blank's beer!"

We shall not give the offending brewery a cheap advt. by repeating the name of the beer mentioned!

A vigorous protest from the Alliance office, over the 'phone, brought forth many apologies from the Manager of the Radio Station, who, of course, said that **he** was not responsible for the wording of the advt., yet he refused the Alliance Secretary the right to tell the public the truth concerning Bradman's courageous total abstinence principles!

AND THE BREWERY?

Yes, a letter was sent to the Brewery concerned complaining of the **shockingly bad sportsmanship** displayed, in capitalising an abstaining champion's name in the interests of beer; but—as we expected—the offending brewery folk had neither the courage nor the courtesy to acknowledge our letter!

WHAT DON BRADMAN DID SAY:

HE PRAISES TOTAL ABSTINENCE.

"Total Abstinence from all Alcoholic Liquors is a big factor in success. Alcohol must necessarily interfere with one's condition, thereby reducing one's power in every direction; so my advice to boys is to leave strong drink alone at all times!"

THE BEST DRINK.

Don has not yielded to the foolish notion that alcohol is a stimulant and useful in a critical situation, for he went on to say:

"The most refreshing beverage of all I find is a cup of tea!"

Printed by The Ruskin Press Pty. Ltd., 123 Latrobe Street, Melbourne, for the Victorian Local Option Alliance, 190-2 Bourke Street, Melbourne.

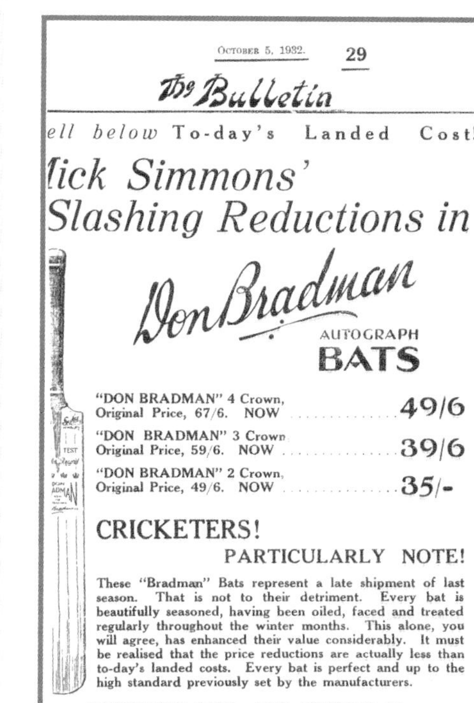

Copy of letter received
from Mr. D. G. Bradman

2nd March, 1934.

To the Manufacturers,
Elasta-Strap Self-Supporting Trousers.

Dear Sirs,

I have just received my Elasta-Strap Trousers for use during the forthcoming English Tour. I am confident that I, and the other members of the Team, will find Elasta-Straps just as satisfactory and helpful as ever. One becomes so accustomed to their great comfort and efficiency that the idea of wearing the old-fashioned style of trousers would never recur. Anything that so contributes to one's comfort, freedom and satisfaction, as Elasta-Straps do, helps strongly to a good performance.

Yours faithfully,

Don Bradman

The original of the above letter may be inspected at the offices of the Manufacturers.

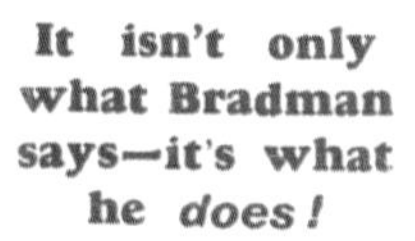

It isn't only what Bradman says—it's what he *does!*

Read This Letter from Don Bradman. . . . It will convince you!

To the Manufacturers,
Elasta-Strap Self-Supporting Trousers.

Dear Sirs,

I have just received my Elasta-Strap Trousers for use during the forthcoming English tour. I am confident that I, and the other members of the team, will find Elasta-Straps just as satisfactory and helpful as ever. One becomes so accustomed to their great comfort and efficiency that the idea of wearing the old-fashioned style of trousers would never recur. Anything that so contributes to one's comfort, freedom and satisfaction as Elasta-Straps do helps strongly to a good performance.

Yours faithfully,

Don Bradman

Champions, at Cricket, Tennis, Golf and Bowls wear Elasta-Straps to their great advantage.

town. When South Australia played in Sydney in a mid-30s Sheffield Shield match soon after his interstate transfer, the 'Bradman Factor' generated 84 per cent of the NSW Cricket Association's revenue for the entire season! Almost 20,000 attended the Saturday's play in anticipation of seeing the game's colossus.

Cricket social historian Richard Cashman reported that throughout the '30s, crowds effectively doubled in Sydney and Melbourne on days the Don batted. Local associations where Bradman was due to play headlined advertising dodgers with 'BRADMAN' in large type and beside his image, in much smaller type, the game itself was advertised. For a generation and more, a Don Bradman waxwork was on display at Madame Tussaud's in London.

He had a Hollywood status every bit as big as any of the movie stars of the day. Despite the adulation and the total lack of anonymity, Bradman remained largely unaffected by the acclaim. He never forgot his elders at Bowral or his friends at the St George Cricket Club, his first major club. Even after he became a member of the Australian Test team, he would wear his St George blazer in preference to his Australian blazer when he visited the club.

He was the white knight of the game, the most marketable figure of them all.

SANFL

CHAPTER TWENTY-THREE

Not everyone's cup of tea

Despite being generally regarded as cricket's divine one, Don Bradman wasn't infallible. His on-field ruthlessness and influence created divisions even within his own teams...

Keith Miller was on the phone. Very excited. He'd been watching Andrew Denton's *Enough Rope* on television.

'Did you see it, Ken?' he began. The voice was unmistakeable.

'Oh, hello, Nugget,' I said. 'See what?'

'My mate "Parky" (Michael Parkinson) was on the telly...last night ... and do you know what? Guess who of all the film stars, personalities and world leaders he'd met and interviewed...guess who he named as his all-time hero?

'Who, Nugget?'

'Me...Me...Little old Nugget.'

The emphasis on the 'ME' was golden. All his woes and ill health were temporarily forgotten. His voice had fire and animation. The recognition and acknowledgment had truly touched him. The charismatic larrikin, everyone's hero of the '40s and '50s, only occasionally left his comfortable little weatherboarder at Mornington. There were times, however, when he made an effort, like St Kilda Football Club's Hall of Fame night and the unveiling of the Miller bronze statue at the MCG, an honour he considered to be among the greatest of his life. 'It was very emotional and moving for him,' said his widow Marie. 'Keith wasn't used to getting great awards. "I'm just

OPPOSITE: the Don stood out in any crowd but not everyone looked at him through rose-colored glasses. Keith Miller, above, was one

The Don with fellow cricketers Bill Johnston, in sunglasses, Keith Miller and Sam Loxton at Colin Hayes' magnificent Lindsay Park stud at Angaston in South Australia

Nugget" he'd say and that's how he truly felt. He didn't talk much about himself.'

Miller hated the restrictions caused by his failing body, but he rarely complained. He'd spend much of his mornings on the telephone to old mates, before a lunchtime snooze, often on the new timber patio Marie had had built.

Once he'd been everyone's hero, the high-flying wartime ace, the devilishly handsome Errol Flynn of cricket, the most charismatic postwar cricketer of them all, who had the widest circle of friends and the common touch to match. Miller couldn't help but be the focus of every conversation. His mates all loved and admired him like no other. The afternoon drinkers and big-noters at Whale Roberts' pub in South Melbourne would suddenly fall silent when Nugget entered. Even footballing great Laurie Nash would take a back seat as Nugget reminisced. They particularly loved the old chestnuts, like the time the '55 boys were in the Caribbean and Miller and fellow prankster Ian Johnson took control of a twin-engine Viking in a memorable joyride between Trinidad and Tobago. It resulted in a stern 'please explain' and the immediate re-writing of board contracts forbidding any player from piloting any plane in which Australian teams were travelling!

While Bradman retreated from public life and refused almost all interviews in his final twenty or so years, there were never enough hours in the day for Nugget. Life was never humdrum for him. He travelled to England for two months each year to visit his bosom buddy Sir Paul Getty at his estate at Buckinghamshire. They'd go to Lord's and it would often take them half an hour to make their way from the members' gates into Sir Paul's private box as Keith would be so busy saying hello to everyone. 'He knew everyone's first name, all the girls, all the gate blokes, everyone,' said Marie. 'It always amazed me, too, how many (MCC) committeemen would suddenly arrive when Keith was there. It was like bees to a honeypot. You couldn't get into Paul's box because there'd be so many of them wanting to say hello.'

Part of Miller's charm was his common touch and knockabout ways. In Johannesburg for the centenary of South African cricket in 1989, he was a shining star in a glittering array of invitees from England and Australia. A bus trip had been organised to show the VIPs the local sights. But after three minutes Keith said 'Stop the bus...Gees, Normie,' he said turning to Norman O'Neill sitting close by, 'what have we got ourselves into here? Let's get off and go and have a few beers.'

Miller was always engaging company and always very generous with his time. We'd known each other for years. When one of my previous books *Wildmen of Cricket* was released (1997), Keith rang and thanked my co-author Brian Hansen and myself for our efforts. 'Ken,' he said, 'the detail you had in there was remarkable. You reminded me of things I'd long forgotten, like my old sportsmaster at Elsternwick, Mr Gainey. I don't know how you got all that, but thank you...thank you very much.'

I told him Brian deserved all the credit. He'd written that particular chapter, in my opinion the very best in the book. 'And by the way, Nugget,' I said, 'We are launching the book next week at one of your favourite watering holes, the Emerald (in South Melbourne)... would you like to come?'

'Sure,' he said, 'I'll come. Who else will be there?'

I reeled off some names and then also mentioned Ian Johnson.

'Oh, Johnno,' he said, his voice dropping. 'You don't want him to come. He'd be boring as hell!' Nugget loved taking the mickey. He thrived on being a larrikin. It was his way. His newspaper stories were always flamboyant and forthright. Some appreciated them more than others. Don Bradman was one who didn't. Miller the columnist went for the jugular. Regularly.

One day Nugget's ghostwriter at *Truth*, Darryl Timms, rang me at

Keith Miller: after the dark war years he felt the Don took the game too seriously

the Brisbane Test and said Nugget had forgotten to file. He had fifteen minutes to get a story into the paper. I was at the game, quickly dictated something and Darryl made his deadline. Twenty-four hours later, Keith duly rang, thanking me for assisting. 'That's the first time I've ever missed a deadline,' he said. We remained mates and when I was writing the history of the St Kilda Cricket Club, *Down at the Junction*, he told me how he should always have played both football and cricket at St Kilda, except he was sent down to the fifth net one pre-season and ended up without any bowlers. 'I was down there again a couple of nights later and one of the players who was a prefect at Melbourne High said to me I was wasting my time down there and suggested I go elsewhere, so I did.'

He became the big fish who escaped and South Melbourne, another of Melbourne's oldest and highest-profiled clubs was to be the beneficiary, Miller excelling in his first game, aged fourteen, against the Saints. Around this time, too, a publisher friend of mine had suggested a book of Miller's career as outlined match-by-match in *Wisden Cricketers' Almanack*, the renowned 'bible' of the game. Would Keith co-operate for an introduction? When I told him a similar book had just been published on Don Bradman, he immediately shook his head and dismissed the idea, totally. 'No, Ken,' he said. 'Not interested.'

When New South Wales released its Team of the Century, Miller, of course, was one of the first chosen. I rang Nugget and said: 'They've got you at No.7 [in the batting order].'

'What…No. 7? Who's at three!' — (knowing full well that that was Don's position).

He'd had a love-hate relationship with Bradman for years, but he'd still ring Bradman on his birthday, wishing him a happy day. 'That was Keith,' said Marie. 'He was a very fair man. He may not always have seen eye to eye with Don on everything, but he knew how much work Don had done for the game. He also appreciated the fact, too, that in '48 Don left the boys alone. There were no curfews. That suited Keith.'

Before the war, representing Victorian against the great South Australian Clarrie Grimmett in Melbourne, Miller hit what he believed to be a bump ball which was taken by Bradman. 'Oh, well bowled, Clarrie,' said the Don and after a delay, Miller was given out, caught. The next day he read an inference that he'd been the subject of gamesmanship.

In Brisbane on his Ashes debut, Miller baulked at banging the ball in short on what was a sticky-dog. He felt he could have genuinely injured someone. Eighteen months later, Miller carried a sore back into the Lord's Test and after Bradman tossed him the ball to bowl, he threw it straight back at him. As historian David Frith said: 'You simply couldn't treat Bradman with such casual disdain — as Miller had with his insubordination and very different lifestyle — and yet expect no comeback.' Miller was as competitive as anybody, but he considered Bradman the captain to be autocratic and ruthless. Cricket, he always said, was a game, not a war. Bradman was too much of a dictator for his liking.

One time in Adelaide he'd been asked by Bradman to a meeting at his Grenfell St office and he hated it, saying he felt like a schoolboy being made to visit his headmaster. The surroundings were stuffy and austere and he couldn't make it back out into the main street again quickly enough. Miller and Bradman were the two beacons of Australian cricket at the time, but were absolute opposites. Miller had somehow survived a war Bradman had been too ill to fight. Dozens of his closest mates had perished. He could easily have died, too.

After all the dark years of the war, it seemed almost surreal to be playing cricket again. He treated it purely as leisure and felt the Don took the game too seriously. He rebelled when Bradman told him to bowl bouncers at opponents like Bill Edrich, who had also just been though the war. Bradman may have been God, but if Nugget didn't want to bowl a bouncer, he wouldn't. Miller felt Bradman was jealous of his wartime exploits and envious of his incredible popularity and ability to mix just as easily with the navvies as he did with nobility. He never truly forgave Bradman, either, for omitting him from the 1949-50 South African tour, a selection sensation as big as any, before or since, despite Miller's early-season declaration that he wanted to be considered for the squad purely as a batsman. Miller felt it was a reprisal for several spur-of-the-moment bouncers he aimed at the Don during a testimonial match in Sydney in 1948-49. Maybe the Lord's incident and others hadn't helped either...

Sam Loxton, Bradman's mate, was at mid-off that late February Saturday when Nugget sauntered by to the top of his run-up. 'Sammy,' he called. 'Think I'll give the little bugger one...don't think he likes 'em.'

Bradman had only just come to the crease. Given that it was his last game at his old home ground, a full one on leg stump to allow the great man a tickled single to backward square would have been a far more diplomatic option. But Keith never cared two hoots for protocol. He accelerated in and let go a bouncer. It was a snorter, too. Bradman had hardly had a bat in his hands since England and the ball all but skimmed his nose. The great man was unamused.

Pleased with himself, Nugget walked past Sam again and said: 'He didn't like that one, Sammy. Think I'll give him another.' By now Loxton's eyes were rolling around in the back of his head. He was horrified. Like the 40,000 fans at the ground that day, Bradman was his hero. In came Miller and banged it in again, short and fast. This time Bradman was ready for it and struck it forward of square like a tracer bullet. It screamed into the mid-wicket boundary just as Miller was completing his follow-through. If the big crowd had been stunned by the first bouncer they were roaring now. 'If the fence and stand hadn't been in the way, the ball would have ended up in George Street, he hit it that hard,' said Loxton. 'It was the best shot I ever saw Bradman play. Miller walked past me again and said: "Okay, I take it all back!"'

Sam Loxton: he loved the Don – he was his hero

Loxton said he knew the two had occasionally disagreed. Asked about the incident when Miller refused to bowl at Lord's in 1948, he said: 'I don't think Bradman had even known he (Miller) had a bad back.' In 1954, Miller seemed to be everyone's choice as Australia's new captain, except for the Don, whose influence was even more marked off the field than it was on.

Colleague Neil Harvey loved the Don like a father but said it was a travesty that Miller hadn't succeeded Lindsay Hassett as Australia's Test captain. 'He was larger than life at the time and simply had everything,' said Harvey. 'But apparently he'd upset the board and that was that.' Bradman always denied being the most influential member of the selection panel. 'There were three men on the panel and three voted,' he said of Miller's controversial omission.

Years later Bradman named the West Indian Garfield Sobers as the finest all-rounder he'd seen, an opinion which further muddied relations. Marie Miller said the pair exchanged phone calls, but there was never the ease and banter her husband shared with his more knockabout buddies.

Miller had refused to be involved with the Australia-wide Invincible reunions but that wasn't any reflection on his sometimes-frac-

tious relationship with Bradman. He simply wasn't one for reunions, even with his old air force mates. He had been prepared to come to Adelaide for the first one, at Government House, where the Don also attended, but had been suffering from abscesses of the shins and sent his apologies 24 hours before the event. He was worried a bump would stop him from going to England, as per normal, for all the partying at Lord's.

Miller lived a roller-coaster of emotions in his last years. He admired Bradman professionally, but they were poles apart in personality. 'That's just the way it is,' he once told me.

MAKING UP

Brian Hansen had sent Keith Miller the page proofs of his chapter for *Wildmen of Cricket* in Sydney and Miller rang, thanking Hansen for his efforts. 'It's the most incisive writing anyone has done on me,' he said. 'I didn't want to be seen to still be feuding with Don

Bill 'Tiger' O'Reilly, en route to South Africa in 1935, and the Don were often on different wave lengths

or be accused of being the boy who killed Bambi. We've made our peace now. You know what I think about Don. He was the greatest cricketer who has ever been, but…'

FULL FRONTAL TIGER

'You don't piss on statues,' Bill 'Tiger' O'Reilly often used to say when talking about the Don. He had strong opinions on everything, particularly Bradman, but he was selective with whom he shared them and even in his autobiography offered only a watered-down view of an enmity which had lingered for years.

They both hailed from the New South Wales bush, but that's where the similarities ended. Unlike Bradman who was quiet, conservative and selective with whom he socialised, O'Reilly was outspoken and gregarious. One year in Brisbane there had been a tropical downpour of such ferocity that play was abandoned early and Tiger, having phoned through his copy, was soon holding court in the Cricketers' Club, a floor down from the press box. Our 'school' started with three and gradually ballooned as the journos, deadlines met, trailed down from upstairs, one by one. Tiger was in his element, telling tale after tale, including one of his favourites when he met the great Henry Lawson one day at White Cliffs. We were all ears. It was rare education. By the time it came for him to shout again, he looked around and said: 'How many is it boys? Nineteen?'

Bradman would never, ever have done that.

Tiger said their differences were all to do with chemistry, arising from their differing backgrounds and they differed, often. Like Miller and Bradman they were to make up, a little, and at the opening of the Sir Donald Bradman Memorial Oval, O'Reilly bowled a ball to the Don. There were smiles and handshakes all round. Years, earlier, though, they had disagreed often, on a myriad of issues as complex as sectarianism all the way through to selection.

Aside from Bradman's refusal to be 'one of the boys', O'Reilly had a genuine beef that the Don, as a first-year captain hadn't backed his players in a hastily arranged meeting with four Board of Control representatives in Melbourne during the 1936-37 Ashes summer. Only the Catholics in the team were asked to attend, O'Reilly, Stan McCabe and Leo O'Brien. A prepared statement was read to the trio which included reference to them as 'boozers and slackers'. The meeting broke up early when O'Reilly, his Irish temper rising, questioned why the trio were there and had the chairman indeed mentioned the words 'insubordination' and 'disloyalty?'

'Are we being accused of that?'

'No, you aren't.'

'Well gentlemen, there is no reason for us to be here,' said O'Reilly and the meeting broke up in confusion, with the chairman still in mid-sentence.

O'Reilly remained bitter that Bradman, a Mason, had not attended to back his players. Religion should never have been allowed to permeate cricket decisions, he said. Weeks earlier in Brisbane, McCabe had threatened to withdraw from the Test when told his wife would not be allowed to sit in the members' stand. O'Reilly was among several who made it known that they would also be joining the McCabes on the train back to Sydney should there not be a reshuffle. Australian authorities were dismayed at the militancy of the players, but Mrs Edna McCabe got to sit in the members'.

Tiger was particularly miffed, too, at his mate Clarrie Grimmett's Ashes series omissions in 1936-37 and 1938. He felt they were 'unpardonable errors' which directly affected Australian performances. He believed Grimmett's toughness, stamina and skill made him essential for six months in England. But O'Reilly never truly explained exactly why he believed Grimmett had been benched until he recorded a series of interviews with John Ringwood for Australia's Oral History Archive shortly before his death, in 1992.

O'Reilly blamed Grimmett's premature exit from international cricket entirely on a throwaway remark Grimmett had made in the South Australian rooms one day after a Bradman century against Victoria. Bradman had survived a fierce attack from Australia's fastest bowler of the time, Ernie McCormick, before late in the day forfeiting his wicket to a loose stroke against part-time leg-spinner Ross Gregory. Grimmett rarely toyed with his words. 'Ha', he said to the Don, as related by O'Reilly. 'You (Bradman) were thinking about the new ball on Monday morning, weren't you? You didn't want to go through it again!

'And they say,' O'Reilly told Ringwood, 'that those ill-chosen words at an ill-chosen moment...brought about the end of Clarrie Grimmett's career.'

Grimmett was like a brother to O'Reilly and for years he targeted Bradman over all sorts of issues via his newspaper columns. 'We had not much in common, not much in common at all,' he told me years later. In retirement, Grimmett always claimed Brad-

OPPOSITE: Clarrie Grimmett was unlucky to miss selection for the tour of England in 1938

man had shortened his international career. He continued to play alongside the Don at Sheffield Shield level and having headed the first-class bowling averages in 1938-39 followed with 73 wickets in nine games for South Australia in 1939-40. Not bad for 48.

ENEMIES FOR LIFE

Another of Bradman's teammates, cricketer-journalist Jack Fingleton, also had an inflammatory relationship with the Don. 'Of all people, the man who nettled me most was Bradman,' Fingleton said in his autobiography, *Batting From Memory*. He accused the Don of being ungenerous and churlish.

When Fingleton was overlooked for the 1934 Ashes tour, he claimed an article by Bradman in the Sydney *Sun* in which he criticised Fingleton's running between wickets had been central in his omission. 'This article from Bradman was hitting a new low,' wrote Fingleton. 'I saw him on the ground floor of the *Sun* just after the team was chosen. I shook him by the hand and wished him good luck. He said "bad luck" to me and I told him: "I think I have largely got you to thank for missing out." '

Years later Fingleton conceded that seven from NSW had been chosen in the touring sixteen. To expect an eighth may have been optimistic. He was to regain his place in the team for the next Ashes summer and in Melbourne during the epic Test of 1936-37 shared in a record stand with Bradman which helped save the Ashes. But the pair were never close. Fingleton accused Bradman of leaking the famous Bill Woodfull bodyline summer quote: 'There are two teams out there. One is playing cricket. The other is not.'

In *Batting from Memory*, Fingleton says Bradman met with Claude Corbett of the Sydney *Sun* that night in Adelaide 'and gave Claude a splendid account of the incident and the words used'. Bradman always denied his part in the leak and said there had been only one professional journalist in the team and that was Fingleton. It inflamed a division which was never to be repaired and in 1978 when Fingleton released a biography of Victor Trumper, Australia's golden age batting immortal, he said Trumper and not Bradman, was the greatest batsman who had ever lived. 'Whereas Bradman ...operated on bowlers like a butcher at the abattoirs, wading deep in their agony and frustration, Trumper was like a surgeon, deftly and classically dissecting everything that was offered against him,' he wrote.

> 'No journalist who valued his survival would write a word against the Don. He was a national treasure and you don't tarnish the gilt of national treasures'
>
> *sportswriter Brian Hansen in his autobiography* The Awful Truth

W. M. WOODFULL

The friction between the pair extended to Fingleton's accusation of Bradman being a strike hog. In *Batting from Memory*, Fingleton said: 'it was not possible to have much of the strike while Bradman was there. He was such a fleet and superb runner between the wickets that he always managed to manipulate the strike.' Ball-by-ball Test records, however, fail to back the Fingleton theory. During the pair's epic partnership in Melbourne, for example, Fingleton received almost 60 per cent of the strike.

Statistician Charles Davis says Fingleton scored slower than most of the front-line Australians and in this case, had he researched a little more diligently, he may not have been quite as scathing in his judgments.

FLYING SOLO

Bradman's teammates, captain Bill Woodfull included, admired Bradman's on-field contributions, but not his habit of 'flying solo'. In an interview years later with R. S. 'Dick' Whitington, Woodfull conceded that Bradman had been 'a lone wolf' in England in 1930, 'not really one of us'. Team relations, too, were further tested when Bradman arrived home earlier than the rest of the team, which had just regained the Ashes. Some accused the Don of deliberately deflecting all the celebratory publicity his way.

Woodfull told Whitington that Bradman's backing-away tactics against Harold Larwood and Bill Voce in the bodyline summer were totally alien to team orders. Whitington quoted him as saying: 'The recognised batsmen were to stand firm behind the flight of the ball when Larwood and Voce were bowling,' he said. 'The plan, agreed to by all except Bradman and followed by all except Bradman, was that we should present a united front...Don was the only batsman to depart from the stipulated policy...for this I can never forgive him.'

Hon: L.H.TENNYSON

MANNERLESS

Former English captain Lionel, Lord Tennyson, the son of a former Australian Governor-General, accused the Don of being 'mannerless' after an apparent Bradman brush-off at Lord's during the '48 tour. He'd been told that Bradman was too busy to see him in the Australian dressing rooms. Tennyson immediately penned a letter and had it delivered to the rooms saying good manners cost nothing. 'I told him I thought that as a former captain of England and the son of a former Governor-General of Australia he might have seen fit to spare me a minute,' said Tennyson. 'I also told him I merely wanted to congratulate him and ask him and Hassett and Brown and Miller to dine with me at the White's Club…'

> '(Denis) Compton is the better cricketer. He has the right outlook. I do not think that he has ever put his own averages in front of that outlook. He remains totally unspoiled by all the honours which have been showered upon him, by the records he has smashed, by the lavish praise the critics have accorded to him. I very much doubt that Bradman has got so much pleasure from cricket, entirely as a game as Compton has done, with, as I write, his cricket career no more than half over'
>
> Former English captain Lord Tennyson (1950)

OPPOSITE, TOP: Australia's captain during the bodyline series, Bill Woodfull, was critical of the Don's technique of backing away

OPPOSITE, BELOW: Lionel, Lord Tennyson was peeved when the Don said he was too busy to see him

TOP: with Denis Compton and Prince Philip

ABOVE: Compton was a pin-up boy for sports-mad England immediately after the Second World War

CHAPTER TWENTY-FOUR

92...OUT

It was the ultimate sporting fairytale...a bush kid's meteoric rise...surpassing the feats of all before him...

Don Bradman, Depression years hero and Australia's ultimate sporting icon, had long been lionised as a legend. Just as he was never dismissed in the 90s during his unparalleled Test career, it seemed inevitable that he would notch another century, the greatest of them all. We truly thought him invincible. The rumours, though, started in Adelaide on a late summer's Saturday in February 2001, that the Don was near death and not expected to see out the weekend.

Less than 24 hours later, on Sunday, February 25, 2001, the prince of all cricketers, the game's ultimate run-maker, an unpretentious and humble man, died peacefully in his sleep at his home at No. 2 Holden St, Kensington Park and a nation stopped.

He'd been battling pneumonia and after being hospitalised before Christmas, had been allowed to return home only under 24-hour nursing care. He'd been bed-ridden for the final week of his life and was so weak and frail he'd been barely able to even talk.

Australia's cricket-loving Prime Minister of the time, John Howard, had been the last person from outside his family to see him. Just over a week earlier, he'd flown to Adelaide to present Sir Donald with an Australian Sports Medal for his achievement and contributions to cricket. The Don had been genuinely touched.

Parliament paused as Mr Howard described the Don as the most dominant figure in Australian history in the 20th century, bigger than any of the most celebrated icons, including Henry Lawson, Howard Florey, Charles Kingsford Smith, Dame Nellie Melba, 'Weary' Dunlop and even Phar Lap. 'He was the ultimate Australian hero, as gracious as he was valiant,' Mr Howard said. 'It is a measure of the Bradman legacy that for two-thirds of the life of our federated nation, Australians have honoured this man like no other. He was the greatest. No one will come near him.'

While not privileged to have seen him play 'live', I, as a young cricket writer learning his trade, was inspired by him.

One of my first books, entitled *Donald Bradman* for school-age children (published in 1983) saw me in regular contact with the Don, then in his 70s. Not only did he offer constructive criticism and ideas for the supplied text, he corrected and edited several sections. In years to come he was to answer dozens of my queries, always replying promptly on his small neat letterhead. Once when the suggestion was made to him that he had been personally responsible for keeping the famous spin bowler Clarrie Grimmett out of the 1938 tour of England, he answered: 'Clarrie was 46. He was finished.'

In a lifetime of collecting, my autographed Bradman books are of particular sentimental value. Not only was Bradman the greatest cricketer of them all, he was a humble and decent man, who into his 80s and beyond answered hundreds of fan-mail letters, signed memorabilia and endorsed the establishment of the celebrated Bradman Museum in his New South Wales home town of Bowral. Captain of the 'Invincibles', the finest cricket team of them all which marched undefeated throughout the 1948 Ashes tour, Bradman created new standards, not only as a player, but as a supreme administrator instrumental in cricket's postwar renaissance.

His life changed irrevocably from the time he made his world record 452 not out for New South Wales in 1929-30, followed just months later by a double century in his fairytale maiden appearance in England at Worcester. The Bradman era provided Australians with their first true sporting super-hero. He made an incredible impact with his phenomenal scores.

During his Test career he made 29 centuries and needed only four runs in his very last innings to finish with a career Test average of 100. He was out for a duck.

Prime Minister Howard described Bradman as the most dominant figure in Australian history in the twentieth century. Opposition leader Kim Beazley said Bradman's passing was like a death in the family.

Bradman's Test average of 99.94 runs per innings during his unparalleled twenty years at the top made him the game's ultimate icon.

Born in Cootamundra and raised in Bowral, Bradman played grade cricket in Sydney with St George before making a century on his Sheffield Shield debut with NSW in 1927-28. In 234 first-class matches until his retirement in 1949, the year he was knighted, Bradman amassed 28,067 runs at an average of 95.14 with 117 centuries, including a highest of 452 not out in 415 minutes. His new world record was to last almost 30 years. He was also a long-serving administrator, a selector and chairman of the Australian Cricket Board of Control.

Persuaded to play one last game, for charity by old friend and the-then Prime Minister Sir Robert Menzies at Canberra's Manuka Oval in 1962-63, Bradman, then 54, made 4 runs. The tributes, messages and reflections at his passing went for days, on radio, television and in the newspapers, the Bradman family being genuinely humbled by the outpouring of emotion, most from people who had never even met him.

Tens of thousands lined Adelaide streets for his funeral, bowing their heads and unashamedly crying as his hearse passed. Respecting the Don's wishes, the funeral ceremony at Adelaide's Centennial Park cemetery was otherwise private, reserved only for the Bradman family and the Don's closest friends. His son, John Bradman, announced that a public memorial service would be held exactly four weeks after his father's death at Adelaide's St Peter's Cathedral, with mourners also accommodated across the road in Adelaide Oval, where giant screens would show proceedings.

The Prime Minister had offered a state funeral, but the Bradman family preferred something more simple and private. The family had been astonished by the reaction to the Don's death and felt the Australian public also deserved their chance to bid farewell. Acknowledging that Sir Donald was 'very much a public figure', despite his distaste for publicity, John Bradman said he hoped the public memorial would be a celebration of his father's life. John Bradman said his father had been 'extraordinarily unspoilt' by his

Still invincible 50 years on, some of the Invincibles and their wives join the Don and the Governor of South Australia for morning tea at Government House in Adelaide, April, 1998: Back row, left to right, His Excellency, Sir Eric Neal, Governor of South Australia, Bill Brown, Ian Johnson, Neil Harvey, Ernie Toshack, Sam Loxton, Bill Johnston, Ron Hamence , Arthur Morris, Doug Ring, Lady Neal.
Front, Barbara Brown, Lal Johnson, Joanna Loxton, Kathleen Toshack, Lesley Ring, the Don, Nora Hamence, Judy Johnston, Judy Morris, Barbara Harvey

fame. 'He remained astonishingly unimpressed by himself,' he said. He described the Don as 'a wonderful father, grandfather and friend. His love, generosity, humour and strong good sense will be very much missed.'

As well as John, Sir Donald was survived by his daughter Shirley and three grandchildren, Greta, Tom and Nicholas. His wife of 65 years, Jessie, Lady Bradman, died in 1997.

In Mumbai, at the start of the first Test between Australia and India, players observed a minute's silence. So did federal parliamentarians — and hundreds of thousands of club cricketers around the country on the following weekend.

His old mate Sam Loxton had visited him the previous autumn. 'It was wonderful,' he said. 'We had an hour and a half together and then he said, "Sammy, I'm tired. I'm going back to bed."'

Bill Brown, for years the oldest living Australian cricketer, said if Bradman really set himself to make a century, hardly any bowler could stop him. Steve Waugh said in 100 years' time, the Don would be as popular as he is today. 'He was a once in a lifetime cricketer, the greatest ever to play the game.' Richie Benaud said he was a visionary, a supreme administrator and as influential a force as cricket has ever seen.

Told by doctors he needed to slow down, Bradman made very few public appearances in the last fifteen years of his life, other than in the committee room at his beloved Adelaide Oval and at notable openings, such as when he was the first inductee into the Confederation of Australian Sport's Hall of Fame in Melbourne in 1988 and eighteen months later when the Bradman Pavilion was opened in Bowral.

At the Confederation Function, he and Lady Bradman were seated beside swimmer Shane Gould, who as a 15-year-old had won three gold medals at the Munich Olympics in 1972, before quitting the sport and living a reclusive life in Western Australia. Gould said she was almost overcome sitting next to such a luminary. 'I knew very little about Don's achievements when the MC presumed everyone knew all his sporting statistics. It was impressive but I was more impressed by Don's dignity, grace and self-assurance than by his cricket scores,' she said. 'He seemed to have risen above the seduction of fame and all of the adulation he had received to maintain his sense of self ... I asked Don for his speech notes so I could reread and savour what he said. He gave them to me, apologising for his messy handwriting on the neatly typed pages. I've still got the speech in my treasure bag.'

Frank Worrell, a remarkable cricketer and magnificent ambassador for the game, was one of the Don's all-time favourites

THE DON RATES SOME GREATS

GEORGE HEADLEY

'I'd class him as a great batsman...he was a very natural player... and he was particularly strong on the leg side.'

BILL PONSFORD

'"Ponny" was a great player in every respect and a great accumulator of runs. He didn't appear to be smashing the bowling to pieces all the time, but nevertheless the runs accumulated and before you knew where you were, you'd find 50 on the board and then 100 on the board. He always gave the impression that he had a very, very broad bat. Clarrie Grimmett reckoned he'd rather bowl to anybody, except Ponsford. He reckoned he was the hardest man of all to get out.'

FRANK WORRELL

'Frank Worrell has been and, in fact, still is a great cricketer in the artistic mould and there aren't very many of them about...we regret deeply that we won't have the pleasure of seeing him again (after the 1960-61 series).'

BOWLER
RUNS
RANGNEKAR
ADHIKARI
KISHENCHAND
GUL MAHOMED
SARWATE 45
NAYUDU 19
HAZARE
AMARNATH 23
MANKAD 43
SOHONI 1 56
INDIA 1 INN 326
AUS 1ST INGS
No OF OVERS 47
BATSMEN
BRADMAN 99
MILLER 63
2 FOR 187
BATSMEN OUT
BROWN 8 1
ROGERS 16 31
WANTED AT
MEMB GATE
SUNDRIES 1
R GRADY
Don Bradman

CHAPTER TWENTY-FIVE

The Don declares

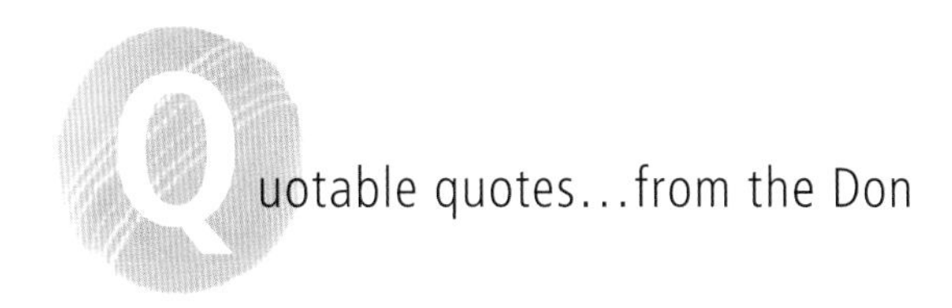

Quotable quotes...from the Don

“No matter how much we love cricket and desire to regard it as a friendly pastime we cannot possibly disassociate its future, at least in the first-class category, from the cold, hard facts of finance,” – *from the Don's article 'Whither Cricket Now', published in* Wisden Cricketers' Almanack *(1939)*

“In 1938 in England I found myself more than once reduced to nine fit men. The tour is a great physical strain for the leading and successful players. Nevertheless cricketers on tour want to play as much as possible,” – *'The Captain's Dilemma', from the* ABC Cricket Book *(1968)*

“Bill O'Reilly was a captain's dream. You could design and place an attacking field secure in the knowledge that he would contain the best of them,” – *from the* ABC Cricket Book *(1968)*

“I was pleased to learn that Allan Border has become the highest scorer in Test cricket. Not only does this recognise his skill as a

Surrounded by young admirers at Melbourne's Spencer Street Station, 1947

batsman, it is also a tribute to his physical fitness and tough character because it has taken many years of toil to reach such a milestone,' – *commenting on Allan Border breaking Sunil Gavaskar's Test runs' record in 1993*

'Genius is unique. If one follows the common pattern one could never be a Trumper whose astonishing strokeplay still thrills the memories of those who saw him,' – *from the Don's foreword to Jack Pollard's* Cricket The Australian Way *(1968 edition)*

'(Neville) Cardus and (Sir Robert) Menzies both had a special eye for beauty as distinct for sheer ability. I knew both men intimately and was enriched by their friendship. It is sad to think we can no longer pick up a morning newspaper and be charmed by a Cardus description of what happened at Lord's the day before. Nor can we put on a dinner suit with the expectation that this evening we shall be thrilled by an after-dinner speech beyond compare by Sir Robert,' – *part of the Don's foreword to* The Natwest Boundary Book *(1988)*

'I feel today amidst all these lights and cameras somewhat like a movie star, of course at a very different salary,' – *an excerpt from one the Don's early after-dinner speeches at the start of what was to become an all-conquering tour in 1948*

'At his best I thought Doug (Wright) had no peer amongst English slow bowlers,' – *the Don, while summarising the 1946-47 Ashes series in* Bradman To Border *(1986)*

'The Lord's Test was a splendid example of the tremendous all-round strength of the 1948 Australians. Every player did something to justify his place in the team and the side just carried too many guns for their opponents,' – *The Don on his '48 Invincibles*

'This innings takes pride of place in my memory bank predominantly because it was without any question the most perfect and satisfying of my life,' – *Bradman referring to his peerless 254 during the 1930 tour in 'The Best Of My 117 Centuries' for* Middle and Leg *(1988)*

‘We saw a truly remarkable display of temperament and concentration by Leonard Hutton...there was scarcely a flaw...throughout the long innings his defence remained impregnable, while all shots were correctly made and every ball played on its merits,’ *– the Don writing about Len Hutton's record 364 in his autobiography* Farewell to Cricket *(1950)*

‘The so-called "killer instinct" is merely a term coined by journalists. I was never conscious of possessing it and frankly I don't think I did,’ *– the Don speaking with Ashley Mallett in* Cricketer *magazine (1974)*

‘Frankly I think it (cricketing superstitions) is so much bunk. In my playing days, the so-called dreaded 87 didn’t exist. Going by the stars, not walking on cracks in the pavement, unlucky 13, not walking under ladders-they all come under the same category – RUBBISH,’ – *the Don again, speaking with Ashley Mallett*

‘My own love of cricket and my enjoyment of it has been enriched enormously through reading the works by writers such as Sir Neville Cardus, H. S. Altham, E. W. Swanton, David Frith, A. A. Thomson, J. M. Kilburn. Ronald Mason, Ray Robinson and many others. My regret is that I didn’t have more time to read before my playing days were over,’ – *the Don in his foreword to David Frith’s* Pageant of Cricket *(1987)*

‘One-day cricket matches appeal to a section of the public and seem destined to play a larger part in our future programs,’
– the Don to journalists after the first one-day international at Melbourne (1971)

‘Come and watch this. You’ll never see anything like it again,’
– Bradman’s call to his teammates in the dressing room from the Trent Bridge balcony during Stan McCabe’s glorious 232 in the 1938 Ashes Test

‘I have never wavered in my contention that the players in the Test arena are merely the display in the shop window. The health and future of the game lies in the hands of the untold numbers of cricket lovers who labour behind the scenes largely unseen and unheard,’
– the Don in his foreword to Geelong’s Blazing Century *(1990)*

‘Don’t worry about it. You’ll find that this is the greatest thing that has ever happened to the game of cricket,’ – *the Don consoling a disappointed Richie Benaud at the end of the tied Test against the West Indies (in 1960)*

‘If ever there’s an occasion for [Ken] Mackay, it’s tomorrow,’
– the Don speaking to West Indian vice-captain Gerry Alexander on the evening prior to the final day of the Adelaide Test when Mackay saved Australia from defeat…from Mike Coward’s Calypso Summer *(2000)*

‘You couldn’t even get Merv Hughes out, you’d be no chance against me,’ – *a classic Bradman quip to West Indian express Patrick Patterson, from an interview in* Wisden Cricket Monthly *(2001)*

‘In the end Australia won the match with 20 minutes to spare but not before we had seen Neil Harvey take an outfield catch which I unhesitatingly rate as the greatest of its kind I have seen. A towering drive seemed certain to go for six, but Neil running flat out to the left, took the catch high above his head and wide on his left side as he jumped feet in the air,’
– *the Don on an exciting climax to the 1948 match against Surrey, from* Farewell to Cricket

With Harold Larwood after the Englishman migrated to Australia in 1950

‘The future of cricket depends on the way our young cricketers cherish and take care of a priceless heritage handed down to them by an imposing array of great – and not so players,’
– *Bradman in the opening chapter to the* MCC Book for the Young Cricketer *(1951)*

‘I saw much better batsmen than I was. Lots of them. They just kept getting out,’ – *The Don explaining his success*

‘He (Shane Warne) is the best thing that has happened to the game for many, many years,’ – *the Don on the emergence of spin bowling sensation Shane Warne.*

DON’S FAVOURITES

Best all-rounder • Garry Sobers
Best batsman • Sachin Tendulkar
Best spin bowler • Bill O’Reilly
Best fast bowler • Harold Larwood
Fastest bowler • Frank Tyson
Best wicketkeeper • Don Tallon

The Advertiser

Adelaide, Tuesday, February 27, 2001 Metropolitan Edition Phone (08) 8206 2000 **90 cents*** including GST

SIR DONALD BRADMAN

1908~2001

Tributes are pouring in from around the world following the death of cricket legend Sir Donald Bradman, Australia's greatest sporting hero.

Reports start Page 2

INSIDE: HIS BRILLIANT CAREER
12-PAGE SPECIAL LIFTOUT

CHAPTER TWENTY-SIX

Tributes, all

From Arlott to Rosenwater, the vote was unanimous, the Don was a genius...

The Advertiser

SPECIAL AFTERNOON EDITION

THE DON DIES

Australia's greatest sportsman, cricket legend Sir Donald Bradman, has died at his Kensington Park home, aged 92.

The director of the Bradman Foundation in Bowral, Mr Richard Mulvaney, said this morning: "Sir Donald Bradman died yesterday morning

INSIDE

Tributes and The Don remembered

peacefully at his home after a short illness with pneumonia."

Sir Donald recently spent several weeks in Calvary Hospital with bouts of pleurisy and pneumonia and had been recuperating at home.

Classifieds Index Page 67 | Call Rhonda on | Metro forecast: Fine, 27 | Index: Page 2

'Excellent timing and wiry wrists invested his strokes with power; his judgment was well nigh perfect, while he was the most relentless punisher of the loose ball — and had the ability to treat even the marginally imperfect ball as loose,' – *John Arlott (1986)*

'He wasn't just a great cricketer; he wasn't just a great businessman, he wasn't just a great supporter of the disabled. He was the greatest man I have known,' – *Dr Donald Beard (2001)*

'There was no one like him and I don't think anyone will be,' – *Alec Bedser (1986)*

'He had a very acute cricketing brain and he was always a couple of overs ahead of the game,' – *Richie Benaud (2001)*

'Bradman was a retiring man. He was a non-smoker and non-drinker. The lounge bar and hotel bar had no appeal to him. He was a good pianist and had a love of good music. He preferred the quiet of

The West Australian

THE DON
1908-2001

A TWELVE-PAGE TRIBUTE TO THE WORLD'S GREATEST BATSMAN

The Advocate

DEATH OF THE DON

Sir Donald Bradman
1908 - 2001

The Advertiser

Farewell The Don

his own bedroom and was quite happy with a gramophone and some classical records. He wrote letters to his girlfriend Jessie Menzies in Bowral and went early to bed,' – *Bill Bowes (1967)*

'At Leeds in 1930, after he had scored 309 in a day, a writer on cricket stated that Bradman had few strokes on the off side in front of the wicket. A diagram of his strokes that day was like the spokes of a bicycle wheel, or rather, like the old advertisements of electric belts with rays of vitality flashing out everywhere,' – *Neville Cardus (1987)*

'He was also, until the end, intensely competitive. Even in his 80s he would come down like a ton of bricks on any bridge-partner who made a mistake. He'd be reluctant to play with them again,' – *Mike Coward (2001)*

'The story of Sir Donald is one to inspire all Australians,'
– *Robert Craddock (2001)*

'Most great batsmen at the end of their careers are able to look back on two perhaps or three truly brilliant innings which are recognised as the high points of their careers. Bradman played innings like this six, seven, eight times a season, year after year,' – *Philip Derriman (1987)*

'Whatever the original limitations of his stroke repertoire, Bradman has become the master of every stroke in the game. But the outstanding quality of his batting skill is that he employs it functionally, ever adjusting to the task at hand,' – *The Hon. H. V. 'Doc' Evatt (1998)*

'There seem no limits to this extraordinary young man's possibilities,' – *Aubrey Faulkner (1930)*

'Bradman is such a curious mixture of brilliant and very mediocre batting,' – *Percy Fender (1929)*

'The entry of Bradman, invariably smiling, sent a thrill round the ground and was greeted in England and Australia with roars of admiration,' – *David Frith (2001)*

'Don was a colossus as far as cricket is concerned. He was the wise man of cricket and was in a class of his own,' – *Tom Graveney (2001)*

THE AGE

BRADMAN: THE FINAL JOURNEY

THE Daily Telegraph

SPECIAL TRIBUTE EDITION

THE DON

1908 2001

16-PAGE PICTURE SOUVENIR INSIDE

'My feet feel tired when I think of him,' – *Joe Hardstaff snr (1994)*

'We approached the dressing room gate and I was still ten metres behind him. Not having played a Test in England before I didn't know what to expect. I had to run as fast as I could to keep up with him,' – *Neil Harvey (2008)*

'Bradman was a great leader. His knowledge of the game is unrivalled and he directed his side on the field with great strategy and understanding. His record as captain speaks for itself,'
– *Harvey again*

'He never gets excited when he scores a century for he can settle down for the second hundred almost as though he had just started his innings,' – *Jack Hobbs (1934)*

'Don's superb skills, his modest courage in the face of great adversity, his unselfish life-long service to the game and to Australia regularly made him Australia's bestknown and most respected citizen in popular polls,' – *Graeme John (2001)*

'It didn't matter what side he was in, he had a huge influence. He was an outstanding player and a very great tactician. I used to discuss things with him about attacking certain batsmen. We didn't have computers to help us in those days. It was all done with the brain,' – *Bill Johnston (1999)*

'Bradman didn't break my heart in 1930. He just made me very, very tired,' – *Harold Larwood (1965)*

'He just wanted to be the best and he was,' – *Bill Lawry (2001)*

'If you think of cricket, you think of Bradman. I would (have) loved to have bowled to him, but I would have had to wear a helmet, – *Dennis Lillee (2001)*

THE EXAMINER

Sir Donald Bradman
1908-2001

THE TRIBUTES: PAGES 2, 10-13

ILLAWARRA
MERCURY

Sir Donald Bradman 1908-2001

The Don is dead

Tributes flow

ILLAWARRA
MERCURY

Sir Donald Bradman 1908-2001

NATION MOURNS THE DON

12-page souvenir liftout

"I want you to know, Ray," he [Bradman] said, "that even if you don't take a wicket beforehand, your place in the Test team is assured. The important thing before the first Test is to concentrate on passing the umpires,"' – *Bradman talking tactics with paceman Ray Lindwall in 1948*

'The Don once picked up a bat in the South Australian dressing rooms and played a shadow cover drive…the bat was a blur, quite unlike anything I had ever seen…never had I seen a bat move so quickly. And he was almost 60 at the time,' – *Ashley Mallett (2001)*

'When you were fielding at the Adelaide Oval, whether it was a Test or a Shield match, you would always look over to the (committee) box to see if he (the Don) was watching,' – *Geoff Marsh (2001)*

'Any shot by Bradman had a better chance of succeeding in its object than any shot made by anyone else, and that it is in fact possible to concede that Bradman's performance was a good deal less risky than it looked,' – *Ronald Mason (1982)*

'It was a great privilege to play for him. He was every boy's hero in the '30s when I started playing. I never dreamt that I would ever be playing under his leadership in a Test match. It's something one could never dream about, let alone expect it to happen. He may not have been as dominating a player after the war as he was before it, but he was still great. He had tremendous natural ability, concentration and determination. He was a wonderful batsman,' – *Arthur Morris (2002)*

'As I look back now and recall my harrowing reactions to my first taste of the killing weight of Bradman's bat, I find it easy to spare a sympathetic thought for all the great bowlers of my time who queued up in their hundreds for a taste of the same medicine,' – *Bill O'Reilly talking of the famous Wingello v Bowral game where Bradman was missed early on his way to 234, all in a day*

'A friend of mine rang me during the afternoon (sometime in 1934) to say that he had just read of Bradman's death on the ticker tape in their busy salesroom…we were in a state of siege with messenger boys chasing us throughout the building to answer phone inquiries, one of which came from Buckingham Palace...The King was deeply concerned about Bradman's condition and wanted to know if his teammates could give him the latest news,' – *Bill O'Reilly again (1985)*

'Poetry and murder lived in him together. He would slice the bowling to ribbons then dance without pity on the corpse,'
– *R. C. Robertson-Glasgow (1949)*

'I have known him for many years and no one I can think of equalled him as a player, as a thinker or as a citizen. He's an astonishing man,'
– *Walter Robins (1998)*

'Don is such a master of back-play that Wilfred Rhodes who bowled against the 'best-ever' batsmen from Grace to Bradman, has classed him as the greatest back-foot player he ever saw,'
– *Ray Robinson (1946)*

'The future student of cricket history may easily be set wondering why Bradman ever got out unless it were from boredom with run making,'– *Robinson again*

'Bradman took batting to its highest pitch. Perhaps only Shakespeare has stood so far ahead of his peers,' – *Peter Roebuck (2001)*

'Sydney forgot its dearer bread, the bitter struggle over the banking bill and that the New South Wales wheat crop was in jeopardy: all went to see Bradman,' – *Irving Rosenwater (1979)*

'Sir Donald had always been and still is on a pedestal — unique and almost god-like,' – *Mark Taylor (1999)*

'Sir Donald is twice as good as the next lot of greats in cricket,'
– *Taylor again (2001)*

'I would consider myself one of the luckiest guys on this Earth to have met the Don,' – *Sachin Tendulkar (1998)*

'Everyone loved Sir Donald Bradman in Australia. He united the country in times of need before and after World War II. He was a great player and inspiration to millions of people including myself,'
– *Steve Waugh (2001)*

SOUTHERN HIGHLAND

Donald George Bradman - August 27, 1908 - February 25, 2001

A Special Tribute to The Don

Herald Sun

DON DIES

The Argus.

Saturday Camera Supplement.

A YOUTHFUL CHAMPION.

CHAPTER TWENTY-SEVEN

How the Invincibles truly rate

Others may have won more Tests in a row, but Don Bradman's postwar teams remain the most celebrated in Australian cricket annals...

No modern-day Australian team, not even the XIs which included Glenn McGrath and Shane Warne, can match the depth of ability or the unbeaten record of Australia's postwar sides dominated by Don Bradman.

Steve Waugh and Ricky Ponting captained teams which won sixteen matches in a row, but neither had a superior unbeaten record to the Australian teams of the late '40s. In the first 25 Tests immediately after the Second World War, the Bradman-dominated Australian XIs won twenty and drew five, the majority against English teams featuring many of the who's who of cricket's finest in Alec Bedser, Len Hutton and Denis Compton.

Ponting's team remained undefeated in 22 matches until 2005 and 2007-08. Old-timers say the disparity between modern Australian teams and the rest is now embarrassing, with only Sri Lanka winning even 50 per cent of their matches in 2006 and 2007.

'We had the best cricket team of all time, bar none,' said Bradman Invincible Neil Harvey.

'They were also the best bunch of blokes you could wish to tour with. Bradman was worth three players alone. There is no player

The 1948 Australians enjoy a light moment as they wait for Ron Hamence to join them for a team photo. The Don seems particularly amused.
Back row, from left, Ray Lindwall, Bill Johnston, Doug Ring, Ernie Toshack, Don Tallon, Keith Miller, Sid Barnes, Colin McCool.
Front, Sam Loxton, Ian Johnson, Neil Harvey, Lindsay Hassett, the Don, Bill Brown, Arthur Morris, Ron Saggers

to compare with him and there is simply not the same competition now.'

Steve Waugh's teams of the early 2000s were also red-hot, winning sixteen and drawing two in an undefeated eighteen-match streak.

The Bradman-led teams of the late'40s had champions at every turn, star openers in Arthur Morris and Sid Barnes, a seasoned pro in Bill Brown, a withering new ball assault led by Ray Lindwall and Keith Miller and emerging youngsters like Harvey, who at nineteen, made a century on his Ashes debut during one of the most famous Tests of all at Old Trafford when Australia ran down 403 on a sixth-day pitch.

The '48 team became the first to remain undefeated through an entire 34-match program, a feat which will probably never be equalled as tours are so much shorter now.

UNDEFEATED AUSTRALIAN TEAMS

Span	Tests	Won	Drawn	% won	Captain (s)
1946-46 to 1950-51	25	20	5	80	Bill Brown/Don Bradman/Lindsay Hassett
2005 to 2007-08	22	20	2	90	Ricky Ponting
1999-00 to 2000-01	18	16	2	88	Steve Waugh
1956-57 to 1959-60	17	12	5	70	Ian Craig/Richie Benaud
Best undefeated run by other teams:					
West Indies 1981-82 to 1984-85					
	27	17	10	62	Clive Lloyd

STAR AUSSIES IN '48

First-class matches

Batsmen	Runs	Ave	100s
Don Bradman	2428	89	11
Lindsay Hassett	1563	74	7
Arthur Morris	1922	71	7
Bill Brown	1448	57	8

Bowlers	Wkts	Ave	Best
Ray Lindwall	86	15	6-14
Bill Johnston	102	16	6-18
Keith Miller	56	17	6-42
Colin McCool	57	17	7-78

First-class matches played:	31
Matches won:	23
Matches Lost:	0
Matches drawn:	8
Test result: Australia	4-0

Ray Lindwall was *the* bowler of the tour with 86 wickets, including 27 in the Tests

"OUR DON BRADMAN"

A Snappy
FOX TROT
SONG

by
JACK O'HAGAN

Written in appreciation of his match-winning and record-breaking efforts.

S/-
2/-

DON BRADMAN ÷ AUSTRALIA'S BATTING PHENOMENON

PHOTO THROUGH CURTESY OF THE MELBOURNE "HERALD".

Obtainable on
Regal Record No. G20744
and Player Rolls

2/- NET

CHAPTER TWENTY-EIGHT

Collecting & the Don

Thousands of memorabilia hunters worldwide queue for Bradman collectibles...

It is 60 years since Don Bradman's last Test, yet the interest in his life and a myriad of mementos and collectibles continues to accelerate. From face masks, gramophone records and sheet music through to photographs, first day covers, coins, badges and books, the race to own something associated with Bradman is big business.

Cricket buffs and collectors looking for alternative streams of investment revenue compete with each other on the internet and through auction houses throughout Britain and Australia. Among the most valuable and prized Bradman items are the authentic pieces from the time:

- a Marylebone Cricket Club tie which sold for $6,000;
- one of his old baggy green caps, auctioned for $23,000;
- or his double century bat from the unforgettable 1936-37 Melbourne Test which made $45,000.

In 1995, noted cricket tragic Mick Jagger of the Rollingstones paid close to $A100,000 for one of the Don's old Australian blazers. Even the incidentals are popular like the Listerine face mask handed out free at the Sydney Test in 1932-33 and the sheet music to the unreleased Bradman piano composition *Every Day is a Rainbow for Me*.

In London, a 1931 release Columbia 78 rpm record, featuring

several Bradman piano solos, preserved in a brown sleeve, sold for $A500, while in Brisbane, two mint condition mono Bradman trade cards produced by the Morrow biscuit and confectionery company made $750 for the pair. No other Australian cigarette or trade card, even the scarce ones from the Federation age 100 years ago command such ever-increasing premiums.

Three delightful flicker books produced in London in 1930, depicting cine-photograph demonstrations of Bradman and his strokes, are also highly collectible. All three can fit in the palm of one's hand. In near mint condition they can command up to $300 per booklet.

The leatherbound edition of Bradman's acclaimed autobiography *Farewell To Cricket* starts at $400. At the time they cost 28 shillings or 30 shillings for the version with the gilt top. The first 150 of the limited edition of 500 were signed and numbered by the Don and at the time available only to members of the London Collector's Book Club. Another Bradman limited-edition also appreciating rapidly is *The Don Meets the Babe* (released initially at around $A75), an account of the 1932 Australian cricket tour of North America, which includes a front cover picture of Bradman shaking hands with baseballing icon Babe Ruth. Signed by the Don, it also includes his lengthy foreword.

The Don also signed the first 200 leatherbound copies of David Frith's monumental *Pageant of Cricket* (1987), just about the most sumptuous limited edition ever released and also one of the most expensive at upwards of $A475. Separately, even unsigned photo-

Don Bradman

D. G. BRADMAN

D.BRADMAN
N.S.W

D. G. BRADMAN.

PLAYER'S CIGARETTES
S.A.C.A.
D. G. BRADMAN

PLAYER'S CIGARETTES
D. G. BRADMAN (N. S. WALES)

CRISPIES WEETIES
VITA-BRITS

MITCHELL'S CIGARETTES
DON BRADMAN

THE
Bradman
LUNCHEON
SEPTEMBER 3, 2002
MCC MEMBERS DINING ROOM

THE
BRADMAN
BOOK
1948
THE STORY AND RECORDS
OF THE WORLD'S GREATEST
CRICKETER.
Compiled by "OUTFIELD"
Drawn by WILL MAHONY
1/-
135
AN ATLAS PUBLICATIO

SIR DONALD BRADMAN
AUTOGRAPH
STIMOROL — THE SPORTSMAN'S GUM

STIMOROL
CHEWING GUM
STRONG TASTE — FRESH BREATH
SIR DONALD BRADMAN
• AUSTRALIA •
D.O.B. — 1908
TEST CAREER — 52
TEST RUNS SCORED — 6996
AVERAGE — 99.94
Acknowledged as the greatest cricketer in the history of the game as his unbelievable average indicates. From 1927 to 1949 he scored 28,067 runs for an overall average of 95.14. He hit 29 test centuries (117 overall) with a highest score of 452 not out for New South Wales against Queensland in the 1929-1930 season. His highest test score was 334 in England (1938). Let's all salute Australia's finest.
© PBL MARKETING
37 of 84

BRADMAN
THE MAN

THE
BRADMAN ERA
RECALLED BY BILL O'REILLY
COMPILED BY JACK EGAN

AWA
CUSTOM
Recording
45 RPM
START OUTSIDE
AW 32952 B.
(AUSTRALIAN)
FREEDOM FROM HUNGER CAMPAIGN)
(5) Margaret Mead 34 Secs.
(6) " " 36 Secs.
(7) David Frost 36 Secs.
(8) Sir D. Bradman 38 Secs.

WISDEN
Cricketers of the Century
Grenada $1
Sir Donald Bradman
Cricketers of the Century
Sir Donald Bradman Sir Garfield Sobers Sir Jack Hobbs Shane Warne Sir Vivian Richards
Sir Donald Bradman

graphs of Bradman playing golf or tennis sell at auction for upwards of $100.

'It's astonishing that a person who hasn't played in his sport for 60 years is still the sports person most in demand anywhere in the world,' said Melbourne-based sporting memorabilia auctioneer Charles Leski. 'The Bradman signature is the most common of cricket signatures. Yet it is also the one everyone wants. The fact that it is common is almost irrelevant. We sell every (Bradman) thing we offer.' Mr Leski said signed autograph sheets especially from the 1930 Ashes tour (Bradman's first) and the 1948 Invincibles tour (his last) can be bought, at a premium. Signed team photos command more than $4000. 'Even blotters and advertising sheets, unsigned and considered rubbish ten and fifteen years ago are going for hundreds of dollars,' he said. 'The tourists would go to a hat factory and everyone would get a hat or a jacket, be photographed and from there the advertising leaflets would be produced. We get bids from everywhere on these. They are genuinely rare.'

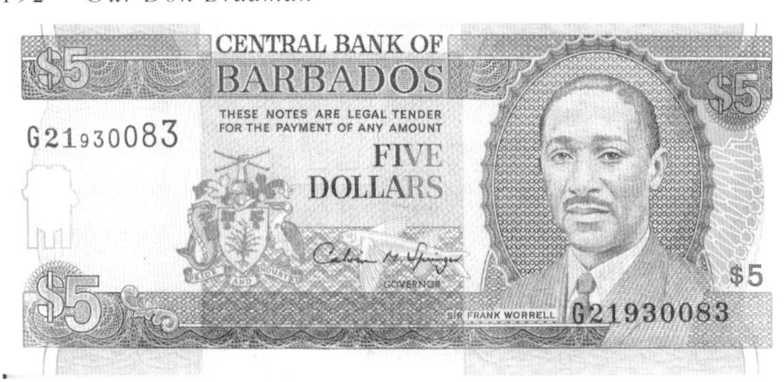

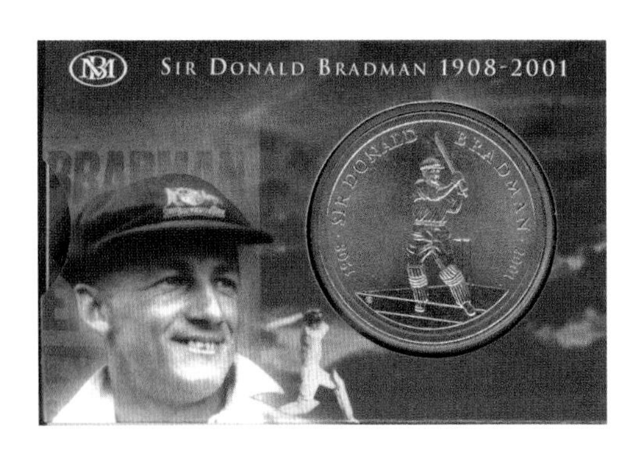

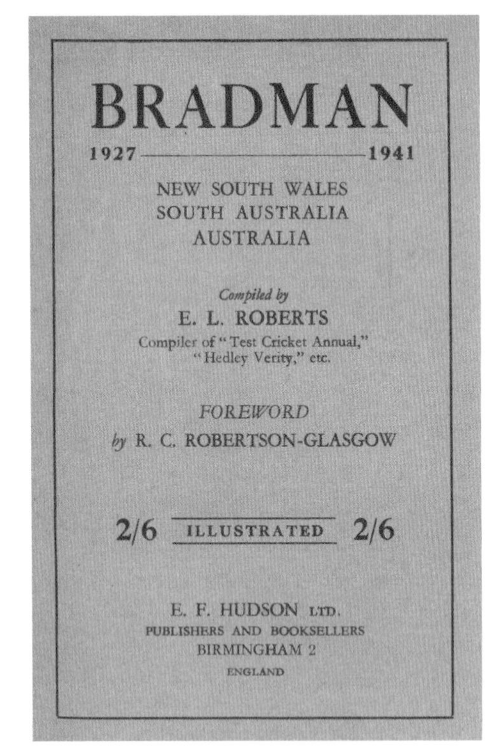

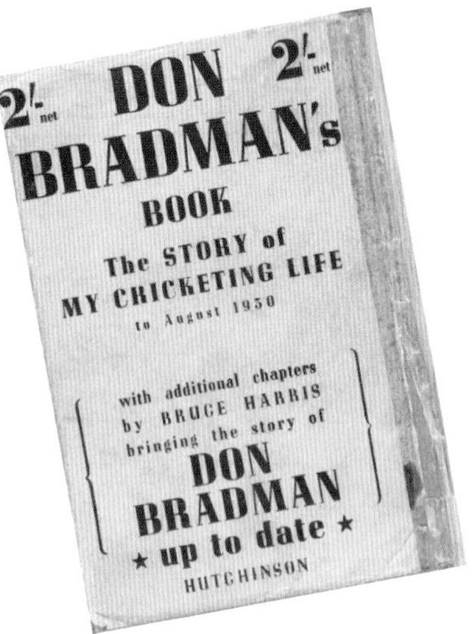

A secondary market is also evolving around reproduced photos, which also include the Bradman signature added sometime in the 1990s. Many of these are marketed by the Bradman Foundation in Bowral, Bradman's old home town, which estimates the potential world market for Bradman memorabilia at almost one billion people.

The Foundation recently approved use of the Bradman name to promote gift-wear, pen and stationary sets and towels. In 2008 a high-quality calendar was produced featuring notable scoresheets from his career. Bradman *Wizard of the Willow* phone cards, the Royal Mint $5 coin series (1996) and Australia Post First Day Covers (1997) also have an immediate market.

In 2002 three commemorative coins were issued in his honor by the Royal Australian Mint and the Perth Mint. They included either an action or a head and shoulders image of Bradman, with the words: 'Sir Donald Bradman 1908-2001'. The three-coin set, limited to 5000, cost $450. While the mintages were high and it was the third Bradman coin issue in five years, they, too, will appreciate in time. The original $5 Bradman aluminum bronze proof coin struck in 1996 sells for up to ten times its issue price.

Until the rush of Bradman coins, no cricketer had been so honored in legal tender terms other than the late West Indian captain Sir Frank Worrell, who, from 1986, has had his image on the $5 Barbados banknote. Previously an illustration of cricket's most legendary nineteenth century player W. G. Grace appeared on a fantasy two shilling banknote used for admission to amusement park Birnbeck Island near Weston-super-Mare in England.

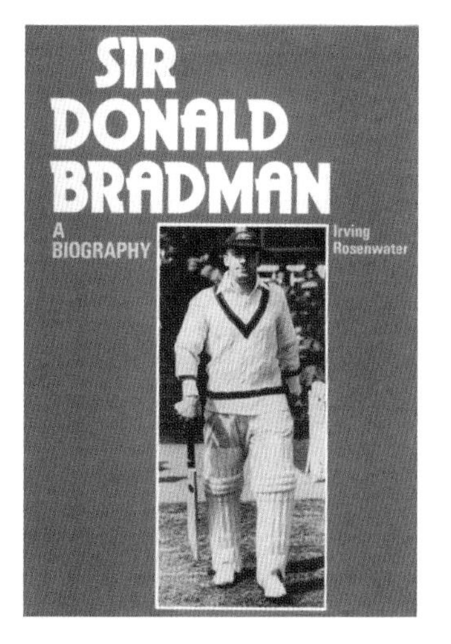
SIR DONALD BRADMAN
A BIOGRAPHY
Irving Rosenwater

FAMOUS AUSTRALIANS
Donald Bradman
KEN PIESSE
HODDER AUSTRALIA SERIES

BRADMAN THE GREAT

Don Bradman's
How to Play
CRICKET
3/-

REMEMBERING BRADMAN
Sir Donald Bradman –
as recalled by those whose lives he touched
MARGARET GEDDES

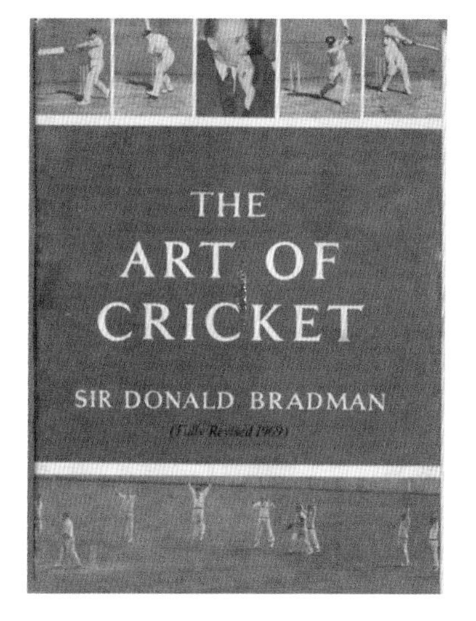
THE ART OF CRICKET
SIR DONALD BRADMAN

Alf Batchelder
Only Yesterday
Don Bradman at the Melbourne Cricket Ground

BRADMAN'S BEST ASHES TEAMS
SIR DONALD BRADMAN'S SELECTION OF THE BEST ASHES TEAMS IN CRICKET HISTORY
ROLAND PERRY

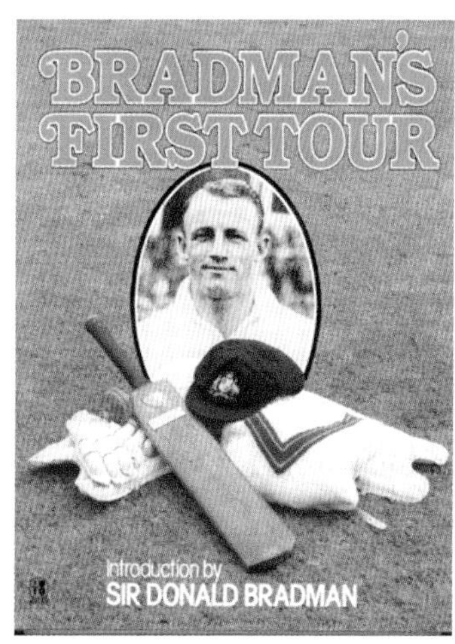
BRADMAN'S FIRST TOUR
Introduction by
SIR DONALD BRADMAN

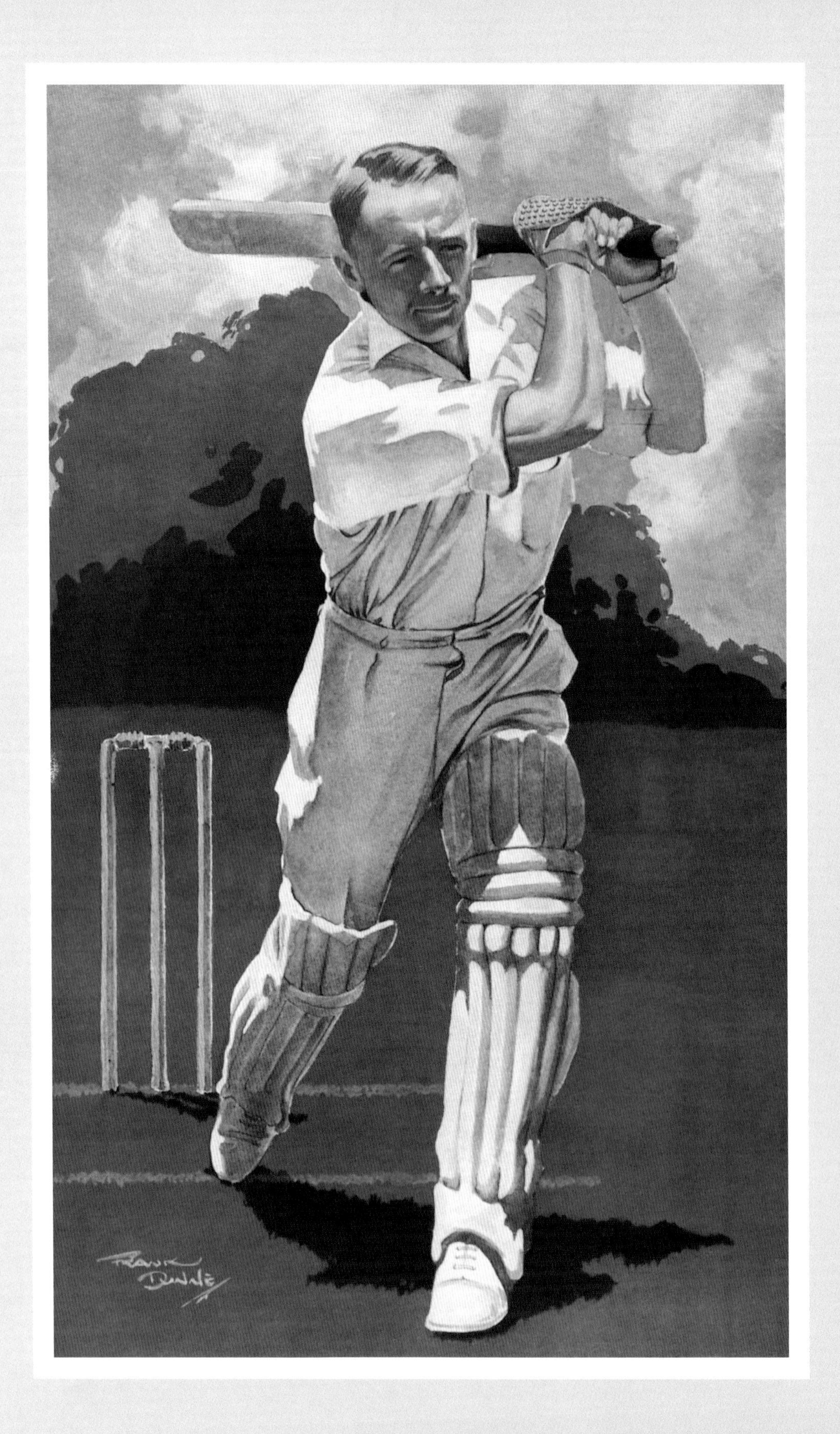
FRANK
DUNNE

CHAPTER TWENTY-NINE

Don's team-mates

Don Bradman had 65 teammates throughout his incomparable twenty-year reign as Australia's outstanding cricketer...

Grenfell's Stan McCabe, with 33 Tests, appeared most often beside the Don in his 52 Test appearances from 1928 to 1948. The brave hero of the first bodyline Test match played some of cricket's finest innings in the 1930s. Wicketkeeper Bert Oldfield was also Bradman's teammate on more than 30 occasions.

The Don's teammates from 1928 to 1948 were:

33 • Stan McCabe

32 • W. A. 'Bert' Oldfield

29 • Bill Woodfull

26 • Clarrie Grimmett

20 • Bill O'Reilly, Bill Ponsford

19 • Alan Kippax

18 • Lindsay Hassett

17 • Tim Wall

16 • Bill Brown

Six of the Don's Test team-mates. From top left, Sid Barnes (in 12 Tests), Bert Oldfield (32), Jack Ryder (4), Harry Alexander (1), Vic Richardson (9) and Ted A'Beckett (4)

15 • Keith Miller

14 • Ray Lindwall, Arthur Morris, Don Tallon

13 • H. 'Bert' Ironmonger

12 • Sid Barnes, Jack Fingleton, Ian Johnson,

11 • Ernie Toshack

10 • Alan Fairfax

9 • Arthur Chipperfield, Bill Johnston, Vic Richardson

8 • Archie Jackson, Colin McCool, Keith Rigg

7 • C. L. 'Jack' Badcock, Len Darling, L. O'B. 'Chuck' Fleetwood-Smith, Ernie McCormick, Ron Oxenham

6 • Percy Hornibrook

4 • Ted A'Beckett, Ben Barnett, Neil Harvey, Sam Loxton, Jack Ryder, Frank Ward

3 • Bruce Dooland, Ron Hamence, H.S. T. L. 'Stork' Hendry, Leo O'Brien, Morrie Sievers, George Tribe

2 • Don Blackie, Ernie Bromley, Ross Gregory, Alec Hurwood, P.K. 'Perka' Lee, Laurie Nash, H. C. 'Slinger' Nitschke, Doug Ring, Merv Waite

1 • Harry Alexander, Hans Ebeling, Fred Freer, Jack Gregory, Merv Harvey, Bill Hunt, Len Johnson, Charles Kelleway, H. S. B. 'Hammy' Love, Ray Robinson, Ron Saggers, H. M. 'Pud' Thurlow

CHAPTER THIRTY

An odd stat or two

Sixty years after his last Test, the Don is still the holder of some remarkable records...

In the world of averages, Don Bradman has gone unchallenged for generations. His Test average of 99.94 is truly spectacular, especially as he played in an era of uncovered wickets. Only one Australian, Mike Hussey, has approached Bradman's average. The pair remain at the head of Test cricket's 'batting order of merit':

	Average
Don Bradman (Australia)	99.94
Mike Hussey (Australia)	78.14*
Graeme Pollock (South Africa)	60.97
George Headley (West Indies)	60.83
Herbert Sutcliffe (England)	60.73

**Figures to March 1, 2008*

OPPOSITE: all eyes on the Don as he leads the Australians out for the last time in a Melbourne Test, 1947

Despite the frequency of modern-day Tests, some of the Don's most spectacular records still top the *Wisden* charts, like his 309 runs in a day and twelve double centuries in Tests. He also scored more than half of his side's runs on five occasions, a tally equalled by only one other, West Indian Brian Lara.

And no Australian has approached Bradman's eighteen scores of 150 or better, or his fabulous first-class record of 117 centuries.

THE DON'S TRIPLE CENTURIES

First-class cricket (6)

340 not out – New South Wales v Victoria, Sydney, 1928-29

452 not out – New South Wales v Queensland Sydney, 1929-30

334 – Australia v England, Headingley, 1930

304 – Australia v England, Headingley, 1934

357 – South Australia v Victoria, Melbourne, 1935-36

369 – South Australia v Tasmania, Adelaide 1935-36

Minor cricket (3)

300 – Bowral Town v Moss Vale, 1925-26

320 not out – Bowral Town v Moss Vale, 1926-27

303 – Kensington v Glenelg, 1939-40

A FAMOUS SOLO

Bradman's highest and most fabulous Test innings is his 334 at Leeds in 1930, a then-record knock which included a century in each session and 309 runs for the day. His first century, before lunch, took 146 balls, a rapid scoring rate, without being extreme in the mould of an Adam Gilchrist. On this day and throughout the entire series, Bradman benefited from a very fast over rate and in that first session, an exceptional share of the strike.

No modern batsman could expect to receive as many balls in a session. During Indian Virender Sehwag's 99 not out before lunch at St Lucia in 2006, the West Indies bowled just 75 balls at him! Bradman's 334 at Leeds outscored the next highest scoring Australian (Alan Kippax with 77) by 257 runs. This 'difference' remains a record for a completed innings.

CENTURIES IN A RUSH

Bradman's fastest Test century came in 98 minutes against South Africa in Melbourne in 1931-32. The number of balls faced is not known — the scorebook is missing — but statistician Charles Davis believes it to be in the 100-110 ball range, similar to the Don's 102-minute century against the West Indies on the same ground the previous season — and which contained his fastest half-century, in 45 minutes.

His fastest 50, in terms of balls faced, was 46 balls on the way to 169 in 1936-37 — once again at his most prolific ground, the Melbourne Cricket Ground.

The Don's fastest double century (in terms of balls faced) was at the Oval in 1934 where he reached 200 off 240 balls, placing him third among Australians, behind Gilchrist (212 balls) and Victor Trumper (233). It is possible that Bradman faced slightly fewer than 240 balls in his double hundred against the West Indies in 1930-31, but the exact number is unknown.

Bradman's 150 in 150 minutes against the West Indies at the MCG ranks third all-time in minutes batted. Ahead of him is Joe Darling with 150 in 135 minutes in 1897-98, and Stan McCabe's 150 in 145 minutes in South Africa in 1935-36.

MASTER CONVERTER

Aside from his unbeaten 103 at the MCG when he ran out of partners in the bodyline summer, Bradman converted seven centuries in a row into 150s between 1931 and 1937. Only one other, India's Sehwag (with eight 'conversions' in succession) has converted more 100s into 150s. South Africa's Gary Kirsten has also made seven in a row.

Of his 29 Test centuries, Bradman reached 150 more than twice as often as he fell short. This ratio represents a huge lead over any other player. The leaders are:

	100s	Out 100-150	150+	Ratio
Don Bradman (Australia)	29	7	18	2.571
Walter Hammond (England)	22	7	10	1.429
Steve Waugh (Australia)	32	10	14	1.400

—Qualification: 15 Test centuries or more

Bradman remains the only Australian to score more than twenty Test centuries without a score in the 90s; although Greg Chappell was never out in the 90s. He, however, did make one score of 98 not out.

FAMOUS SOLOS

In their first ever Test against Australia, at the 'Gabba in 1947-48, the Indians copped a memorable drubbing from Bradman. Bradman scored 185 and India was bowled out for 58 and 98, thereby 'losing' to the Don by an innings! Englishishmen Len Hutton (in 1938) and Bobby Abel (1889) are the only other batsmen who, in a single innings, totally outscored their opponents in a completed match.

200 IN THE SECOND INNINGS

Bradman remained, for several generations, the only Australian to make a Test double century in the second innings of a match, a feat that he registered in consecutive Tests in Melbourne (270) and Adelaide (212) in his first season as captain in 1936-37. This was finally emulated by Victorian Brad Hodge against South Africa in 2005-06.

MOST RUNS IN HIS SECOND TEST

Bradman's failures in his first Test (18 & 1) and his last (0) are well known, but it is much less well-known that Bradman holds the Australian records for most runs in both his second Test and in his second-last Test matches.

In his second Test he scored 191 runs (79 & 112) at the MCG in 1928, ahead of Ross Edwards' 183 at Nottingham in 1972, while his 206 runs at Leeds in 1948 (33 & 173 not out) in his second-last Test beats Bill Ponsford's 181 at the Oval in 1934.

The most runs by any player in his second Test is 274 by Zaheer Abbas of Pakistan, and in a second-last Test, 296 by Eric Rowan of South Africa.

Australians Neil Harvey and Bill Ponsford and England's F. S. Jackson are the only other batsmen to score centuries in both their second Test and penultimate Test matches.

COLOMBO ONE-DAYERS

Don Bradman's career ended long before the first official one-day international. Yet Bradman did play in one-day internationals, of a sort. On a number of occasions, Australian touring teams on their way to England stopped off in Colombo and played one-day games against Ceylonese representative sides; the earliest was a one-day game in 1930 when Bradman scored 40. He also played in Colombo in 1948 but found the heat oppressive and was out for 20. The Australians batted for 75 overs in the first one-dayer and 60 in the second.

WORKLOAD

Today's international schedule is frenetic. Just how does the amount of cricket played by today's players compare to earlier eras?

Players like Adam Gilchrist and Ricky Ponting averaged around 100 days of cricket per year at their peak. Mark Waugh averaged 114 days per year in the mid-1990s and Allan Border 108 days per year in the late-1980s.

Don Bradman averaged about 60 days per year of first-class and Test cricket early in his career; in 1928-29, including his club appearances, too, he played on 68 days, an amazing amount for a man holding down a full-time job.

Interstate travel, too, was then by steam train. When the teams toured overseas they went by ship. Today's professionals play between 40 and 60 days in an Australian season.

A day's play in Bradman's time, especially in England, consisted of around 140 overs; now there is 90 and sometimes less.

KING OF THE BBDs

Bradman dominates most charts, even the 'Balls Between Dismissals' (BBD), the average number of balls a batsman receives in-between dismissals. His lead, however, is slim.

Bradman has a 'BBD' of 164 balls, only marginally ahead of England's Herbert Sutcliffe on 163. Australia's Mike Hussey has also started his career with a BBD of almost 150. Another Australian, Sid Barnes, South Africa's Bruce Mitchell and West Indian George Headley have BBDs over 150. Bradman's BBD 'lead' is so much smaller than his lead in the batting averages as he tended to score so quickly, at 61 runs per 100 balls, an exceptionally high ratio by the standards of his time. Sutcliffe may have batted for almost as long as the Don, but he scored at just 37 runs per 100 balls.

BOUNDARY RECORDS

Bradman's 46 boundaries at Leeds in 1930 remains an Ashes record. Matthew Hayden eclipsed his boundary hits record with 38 fours and 11 sixes in his record 380 against Zimbabwe in Perth in 2003-04. More surprisingly, Bradman once reached a century with only two boundaries, on the way to 144 not out at Nottingham in 1938. This equals the fewest by any Australian, alongside a Bill Woodfull century in 1931-32. The only batsman with fewer boundaries is England's Graham Thorpe, who reached a century with just one four in Pakistan in 2000.

KEY CONTRIBUTOR

In Tests involving Bradman before the Second World War, Australia only twice reached 400 without a significant contribution from the Don. At Manchester in 1934, Australia scored 491 with Brad-

BALLS FACED PER DISMISSAL

	Span	Career Runs	Runs/ 100 balls	BBD
1 • D. G. Bradman (Australia)	1928-1948	6996	61.1	164
2 • H. Sutcliffe (England)	1924-1935	4555	37-38	163
3 • S. G. Barnes (Ausralia)	1938-1948	1072	41.3	153
4 • B. Mitchell (South Africa)	1929-1949	3471	31-32	151
5 • G. A. Headley (West Indies)	1930-1954	2190	44-45	150
6 • M. E. K. Hussey* (Australia)	2005-	2188	52.2	148
7 • L. Hutton (England)	1937-1955	6971	38-39	147
8 • D. R. Jardine (Eng)land	1928-1934	1296	32-33	146
9 • K. F. Barrington (Engand)	1955-1968	6806	41-42	143
10 • C. A. Davis (West Indies)	1968-1973	1301	38-39	143

* To 1 March, 2008

CORNERING THE STRIKE

Where records survive, Bradman averaged 51-52 per cent of the strike with all partners. The slight excess above 50 per cent can partly be put down to Bradman's batting with tailenders, when he was within his rights to manipulate the strike.

In his two mega partnerships with Bill Ponsford in 1934, Bradman received 50.8 per cent of the strike.

man making 30 and at Lord's in 1938, Australia scored 422 with Bradman out for 18.

35 CENTURY STANDS

Bradman was involved in 35 century partnerships during his Test career, and these partnerships averaged a remarkable 204 runs, 50 runs more than a typical century stand at the time. Every one of Bradman's first ten Test century partnerships were worth 150-plus. Bradman dominated the scoring in nearly all of his century stands; despite receiving only 49 per cent of the strike (in century stands in Ashes Tests), he scored just over 60 per cent of the runs off the bat. His scoring rate of 65 runs per 100 balls completely overshadowed his partners, who on average scored at 41 runs per 100 balls.

No one outscored Bradman in a major partnership until Trent Bridge in 1938, when Bill Brown made 91 in a partnership of 172 with the Don.

THE TRUTH ABOUT THE 234s

Sid Barnes' epic Ashes partnership with Bradman, 405 for the fifth wicket at Sydney in 1946, spanned 805 balls, the longest partnership by Australian batsmen by a margin of just one ball — ahead of the Bradman and Ponsford stand of 388 (from 804 balls in 1934). When Bradman was finally out for 234, Barnes famously threw his wicket away next over when on the same score, saying later that he thought his innings would be remembered longer if his score was the same as Don's. Ironically, in a surviving scorebook of this Test, Barnes' scoring strokes add up to 233! But a closer look at the bowling analyses of this score reveals a single to Barnes that was missed in the batting section. His 234 still stands.

BRADMANIA

The memorable Ashes summer of 2006-07 set new records for attendances in internationals, with 813,000 witnessing the Tests and 426,000 watching the one-day internationals. However, the season's Tests crowd aggregate fell short of the Bradmania-fuelled seasons of 1946-47 (when 847,000 came) and 1936-37 (949,000).

In terms of intensity of public interest (in a much smaller population), that era will remain Australian cricket's high point, but the recent season did surpass them in terms of daily average crowds.

Tests were longer back then, so the 1936-37 record was spread over 26 days at an average of 36,500 per day, compared with 22 in 2006-07 at an average of 37,000 per day.

IN THE FIELD

Bradman was an athletic and outstanding cover fieldsman, especially pre-war. In his first series in 1928-29, he became the only fieldsman to run out one of his heroes, England's Jack Hobbs. Hobbs returned the favour at a critical moment later in the series and remained the only man to run Bradman out in a Test. Bradman went on to effect nine run-outs in Tests, well short of Hobbs' record of (at least) nineteen, but few other non-keepers have exceeded Bradman's haul without playing a huge number of Tests (Ricky Ponting, for example, ran out eleven batsmen in his first 116 Tests).

While he was run out only once, Bradman did see partners run out on six occasions, mostly in his first years in the Test team.

MOST CENTURY STANDS IN TESTS

Ricky Ponting • 65*
Steve Waugh • 64
Allan Border • 63
Justin Langer • 50
Matthew Hayden • 49*
Mark Waugh • 47
Greg Chappell • 44
David Boon • 42
Mark Taylor • 40
Don Bradman • 35
Neil Harvey • 33

* To 1 March 2008

THE DON IN TEST CRICKET

Season	Opponent	Mts	Inns	NO	Runs	HS	Ave	100s
1928-29	England (h)	4	8	1	468	123	66.86	2
1930	England (a)	5	7	0	974	334	139.14	4
1930-31	West Indies (h)	5	6	0	447	223	74.50	2
1931-32	South Africa (h)	5	5	1	806	299*	201.50	4
1932-33	England (h)	4	8	1	396	103*	56.57	1
1934	England (h)	5	8	0	758	304	94.75	2
1936-37	England (h)	5	9	0	810	270	90.00	3
1938	England (h)	4	6	2	434	144*	108.50	3
1946-47	England (h)	5	8	1	680	234	97.14	2
1947-48	India (h)	5	6	2	715	201	178.75	4
1948	England (h)	5	9	2	508	173*	72.57	2
Total		52	80	10	6996	234	99.94	29

BOOKS
Andrews, Bill, *The Hand That Bowled Bradman, memories of a professional cricketer*, Macdonald, London, 1973
Arlott, John (ed.), *Cricket: The Great Ones*, Pelham Books, London, 1967
Arlott, John, *100 Greatest Batsmen*, Queen Anne Press, London, 1986
Bedser, Alec, *Twin ambitions, an autobiography*, Stanley Paul, London, 1986
Bradman, Don, Farewell to Cricket, Hodder and Stoughton, London, 1950
Cardus, Sir Neville, *Australian Summer*, Souvenir Press, London, 1987
Cashman, Richard, *Ave a Go Yer Mug! Australian cricket crowds from larrikin to occer*, Collins, Sydney, 1984
Compton, Denis, *Compton on Cricketers Past and Present*, Cassell, London, 1980
Coward, Mike, *Calypso Summer*, ABC Books, Sydney, 2000
Derriman, Philip (ed.), *Our Don Bradman*, Macmillan, Melbourne, 1987
Derriman, Philip, *The Top 100*, Fairfax Library, Sydney, 1987
Eason, Alan, *The A to Z of Bradman*, self published, Sydney, 2002
Edrich, W. J. 'Bill', *Cricket Heritage*, Stanley Paul, London, 1948
Engel, Matthew (ed.), *The Guardian Book of Cricket*, Pavilion Books, London, 1986
Fender, Percy, *The Turn of the Wheel*, Faber and Faber, London, 1929
Fingleton, Jack, *Batting From Memory*, Collins, Sydney, 1981
Frewin, Leslie (ed.), *The Natwest Boundary Book*, Macmillan, Melbourne, 1988)
Frith, David, *Pageant of Cricket*, Macmillan, Melbourne, 1987
Geddes, Margaret, *Remembering Bradman*, Penguin Australia, Melbourne, 2002
Gibbs, Stephen W., *The Don: a bibliographical & referential journey*, self-published, Sydney, 2005
Hansen, Brian, *The Awful Truth, the inside story of crime and sport*, Brian Hansen Publications, Bentleigh, 2004
Hele, George & Whitington, R. S. 'Dick', *Bodyline Umpire*, Rigby, Adelaide, 1974
James, Alfred, *The Don vs The Rest, the scorecards of the minor cricket matches played by Sir Donald Bradman, 1920/21 to 1962/63*, self-published, Sydney, 2006
Kippax, Alan (in collaboration with Barbour, Eric), *Anti Body-line*, The Sydney & Melbourne Publishing Co., Sydney, 1933
Lindwall, Ray, *Flying Stumps*, Stanley Paul, London, 1954
Lodge, Derek, *D. G. Bradman, his record innings-by-innings, Famous Cricketers Series No.32*, Association of Cricket Statisticians and Historians, Nottingham, 1996
Mason, Ronald, *Ashes In The Mouth*, The Hambledon Press, London, 1982
McGilvray, Alan (foreword), *Bradman To Border*, ABC Books, Sydney, 1986
Morris, Barry (ed.), *Bradman What They said About Him*, ABC Books, Sydney, 1994
Moyes, A. G. 'Johnnie', *Bradman*, Angus and Robertson, Sydney, 1948
O'Dowd, Kevin, *Geelong's Blazing Century*, privately published, Geelong, 1990
O'Reilly, Bill, Tiger, *60 years in cricket*, Collins, Sydney, 1985
Page, Michael, *Bradman the Illustrated Biography*, Macmillan, Sydney, 1983
Perry, Roland, *Bradman's Best, Sir Donald Bradman's selection of the best team in cricket history*, Random House Australia, Sydney, 2001
Piesse, Ken, *Donald Bradman, Famous Australians*, Hodder Australia, Sydney, 1983
Piesse, Ken, *Cricket's Colosseum, 125 years of Test cricket at the Melbourne Cricket Ground*, Hardie Grant Books, Melbourne, 2003
Pollard, Jack, *Cricket The Australian Way*, Lansdowne Press, Melbourne, 1968 edition
Pollard, Jack (ed.), *Middle and Leg*, Macmillan, Melbourne, 1988
Robinson, Ray, *Between Wickets*, Collins, London, 1946
Robinson, Ray, *On Top Down Under*, Cassell, Melbourne, 1975
Rosenwater, Irving, *Sir Donald Bradman, a biography*, B. T. Batsford Ltd., London, 1978
Smith, Wayne, *A Superb Century, 100 Years of the Gabba 1895-1995*, Focus Publishing, Sydney, 1995
Sissons, Ric, *The Don Meets the Babe*, J. W. McKenzie, London, 1995
St John , John (ed.), *The MCC Book for the Young Cricketer*, Naldrett Press, London, 1951
Tennyson, Lionel Lord, *Sticky Wickets*, Christopher Johnson, London, 1950
Swanton, E. W. 'Jim' with Rayvern Allen, David, *Last Over*, Richard Cohen Books, London, 1996
Wakley, B. J., *Bradman The Great*, Nicholas Kaye & Co., London, 1959
Whitington, R. S. 'Dick', *Simpson's Safari, South African Test Series 1966-67*, William Heinemann, London, 1967
Williams, Charles, *Bradman*, Abacus, London, 1997
Wright, Graeme (ed.), *Wisden on Bradman, 90th Birthday Edition*, Hardie Grant Books, Melbourne, 1998

NEWSPAPERS
The Advertiser
The Age
The Australian
The Daily Telegraph

MAGAZINES
ABC Cricket Book
Australian Cricket Yearbook
Cricketer
Pavilion, magazine of The Australian Cricket Society Inc.
Sporting Life
The Cricketer International
Wisden Cricket Monthly
Wisden Cricketers' Almanack

VIDEO
Jack Egan, *The Story of Cricket In Australia* (ABC, 1987)

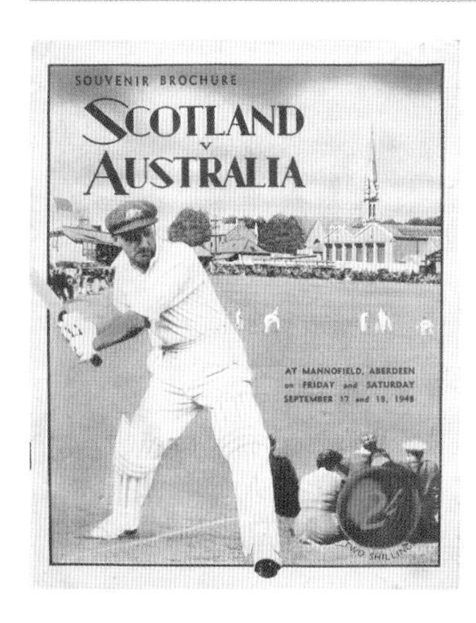

A'Beckett, Ted 196
Abel, Bobby 201
Alexander, Gerry 174, 196
Allen, G. O. 'Gubby' 66, 106
Alley, Bill 125
Altham, H. S. 'Harry' 174
Andrews, Bill 105
Andrews, Tommy 29
Arlott, John 142, 177
Armstrong, Warwick 37, 38
Astor, Mary 50

Badcock, C. L. 'Jack' 196
Barnes, Sid 125-130, 184, 196, 203, 204
Barnes, Sydney 106
Barnett, Ben 126, 196
Barrow, Ivan 105
Beard, Dr Don 177
Beazley, Kim 167
Bettington, Dr Reg 57
Bedser, Alec 106, 109, 142, 177, 183
Bell, A. J. 'Sandy' 135
Benaud, Richie 117, 125, 129, 166, 174, 177
Black, Bill 113
Blackie, Don 196
Border, Allan 101, 118, 171-172, 202
Bowes, Bill 55, 61, 106, 136-137, 177-178
Bowley, Bruce 114
Bradman, Emily 19, 46-47
Bradman, George 19, 21
Bradman, Jessie (nee Menzies) 50, 62, 75, 76, 89, 93-95, 100-101, 104, 109, 120, 168
Bradman, John 75, 76, 77, 94, 97, 98, 168
Bradman, Ross 94
Bradman, Shirley 94, 168
Bradman, Vic 94
Bromley, Ernie 196
Brown, W. A. 'Bill' 69, 111-112, 126, 162, 184, 195, 204
Bunt, Oscar 105
Burke, Jimmy 128

Cardus, Sir Neville 134, 137, 139, 172, 174, 178
Carmody, Keith 59
Carter, Hanson 50
Cashman, Richard 149
Chapman, Percy 134
Chappell, Greg 101, 117-118, 201
Chappell, Ian 117
Chappell, Trevor 100
Chipperfield, Arthur 196
Churchill, Winston 63
Clarke, Michael 120
Compton, Denis 40, 143, 183
Corbett, Claude 161
Coward, Mike 178
Cowper, Bob 135
Craddock, Robert 178
Cumming, Ken 126

Darling, Joe 200
Darling, Len 196
Davidson, Hughie 40
Davis, Charles 39, 40, 107, 162, 200
De Courcy, Jim 129
Denton, Andrew 151
Derriman, Philip 39, 178
Dewes, John 116
Donnan, Harry 27
Dooland, Bruce 126, 196
Douglas, Johnny 67
Duleepsinhji, K.S. 134
Dunlop, E. 'Weary' 168
Dunstan, Keith 66
Dwyer, E. A. 'Chappie' 123-131
Dyson, John 118-119

Ebeling, Hans 196
Eccles, Graham 120-121
Edrich, Bill 77, 155
Edwards, Ross 202
Evans, Godfrey 143
Evatt, The Hon. H. V. 'Doc' 178

Fairfax, Alan 133, 196
Farnes, Kenneth 69
Faulkner, Aubrey 178
Fender, Percy 44, 178
Fingleton, Jack 67, 76, 90, 112, 124, 127, 141, 196
346 run stand with the Don 138
Inflammatory relationship with the Don 161-162
Rates Trumper the Don's superior 161
Fleetwood-Smith, L. O'B. 'Chuck' 50, 66, 67, 72, 196
Florey, Howard 166
Fothergill, Des 125-126
Freer, Fred 196
Frith, David 137, 155, 174, 178, 188
Fry, C. B. 72, 125

Gable, Clark 50
Gavaskar, Sunil 109, 172
Geddes, Margaret 114
Getty, Sir Paul 153
Gilbert, Eddie 107
Gilchrist, Adam 200, 202
Gleeson, John 119
Gough, Frank 29
Gould, Shane 168-169
Grace, Dr. W. G. 19, 39-40, 192
Graveney, Tom 179
Gregory, Jack 27, 35, 196
Gregory, Ross 106, 159, 196
Griffith, Herman 106
Grimmett, Clarrie 27, 35, 109, 129, 135, 137, 154, 159-160, 195
'Finished in 1938' 166

Hamence, Ron 81, 196
Hammond, Jeff 118
Hammond, Walter 31, 33, 67, 76, 105, 108, 201
Critical of the Don 77
Hansen, Brian 153, 157
Hardstaff, Joe snr 179
Harlow, Jean 50
Harris, Gordon 37
Harvey, Merv 126, 196
Harvey, Neil 87, 101, 125, 143, 156, 175, 179, 183-184, 196, 202
Hassett, Lindsay 59, 80, 126, 141, 156, 162, 195
Hayden, Matthew 203
Headley, George 169, 199, 203
Healy, Ian 101, 120
Hele, George 57
Hendren, E. H. 'Patsy' 29, 67
Hendry, H. S. T. L. 'Stork' 196
Hill, Clem 67, 108
Hobbs, Jack 31, 37, 38, 66, 67, 106, 141, 179, 205
Hodge, Brad 201
Hodgetts, Harry 65, 76, 97
Hole, Graeme 128-129
Hollies, Eric 81, 106, 108, 116
Hookes, David 118
Hornibrook, Percy 196
Howard, John 165-168
Hughes, Merv 174
Hunt, Bill 196
Hurwood, Alec 39, 196
Hussey, Mike 199, 203
Hutcheon, Jack 35
Hutton, Len 71, 89, 106, 173, 183, 201

Ikin, Jack 76-77
Ironmonger, Bert 'Dainty' 56, 106, 107-108, 196

Jackson, Archie 27, 196
Jackson, F. S. 202
Jagger, Mick 187
James, Alf 97
Jardine, Douglas 53-57, 59, 61, 95, 108
Jenner, Terry 118
John, Graeme 179
Johnson, Ian 'Johnno' 152, 153, 196
Johnson, Len 196
Johnston, W. A. 'Big Bill' 76, 79, 83, 114-115, 126, 179, 196

Karloff, Boris 50
Kelleway, Charles 35, 196
Kilburn, J. M. 174
King George V 46
Kingsford Smith, Charles 166
Kippax, Alan 27, 40, 50, 106, 135, 195, 200
Kirsten, Gary 201
Kishenchand, Gogumai 105

Laker, Jim 79, 142
Langley, Gil 127
Lara, Brian 40, 199
Larwood, Harold 38, 53, 55-57, 61, 89, 137, 162, 175, 179
Laumen, Louis 109
Lawry, Bill 120, 125, 179
Lawson, Henry 158, 168
Lee, P. K. 'Perka' 196
Lee, Terry 117
Leski, Charles 191
Lillee, Dennis 101, 107, 109, 125, 179
Lindrum, Walter 50
Lindwall, Ray 76, 79, 101, 109, 128, 180, 184, 196
Love, H. S. B. 'Hammy' 27, 196
Loxton, Sam 118, 125, 155, 156, 166, 196
Loye, Myrna 50

Macartney, Charlie 24-25, 27, 40, 104
Mackay, Ken 174
Mailer, Dr Ramsay 107
Mailey, Arthur 29
  Private tour of USA and Canada 50-51, 65, 113
Mallett, Ashley 173, 174, 180
Marsh, Geoff 180
Martin, Ray 93, 101
Mason, Ronald 174, 180
May, Norman 101
McCabe, Stan 29, 40, 50, 66, 106, 158, 159, 200
  Trent Bridge masterpiece 174
  Most Tests alongside the Don 195
McCool, Colin 115, 196
McCormick, Ernie 114, 159, 196
McDonald, Colin 128
McGrath, Glenn 183
McKenzie, Graham 120
Meckiff, Ian 'Mecko' 117
Melba, Dame Nellie 166
Menzies, Sir Robert 108, 116, 167, 172
Menzies, Roy 94
Meuleman, Ken 125
Miller, Keith 'Nugget' 59, 76, 79, 101, 106, 107, 117, 119, 120, 123, 124, 126, 128, 131, 162, 184, 196
  Love-hate relationship with the Don 151-158
Miller, Marie 151-156
Mitchell, Bruce 203
Moroney, Jack 128
Morris, Arthur 59, 80-83, 101, 109, 141, 143, 180, 184, 196
Moulton, Dick 114
Moyes, A. G. 'Johnnie' 25

Nash, Laurie 152, 196
Nitschke, H. C. 'Slinger' 196
Nothling, Otto 35-36

O'Brien, Leo 56, 136, 158, 196
Oldfield, W. A. 'Bert' 55, 106, 195
O'Neill, Norman 153
O'Reilly, W. J. 'Tiger' 23, 55, 67, 69, 101, 109, 123, 124, 126, 127, 129, 135, 137, 141, 175, 180-181, 195
  Blamed the Don over Grimmett's exit 159-160
  Hauled in front of Board 158-159
  'A captain's dream…' 171
Oxenham, Ron 37, 196
Oxlade, Aubrey 125

Packer, Kerry 100
Page, Michael 138
Parkinson, Michael 151
Patterson, Patrick 175
Perry, Roland 109
Pickett, Ted 112-113
Piesse, K. C. 'Ken' 115-116
Piesse, P. A. R. 'Pat' 115-116
Piesse, R. L. 'Bob' 72-73
Pollard, Jack 172
Pollock, Graeme 199
Ponsford, Bill 38-39, 43, 56, 101, 107, 120, 134, 135, 195, 202, 204
  Comparison with the Don 49
  451 run stand with The Don 137
  Don's opinion of him 169
Ponting, Ricky 120, 183, 202, 205
Puckett, Charlie 126

Quin, Stan 66
Quinn, Neville 50

Rainsbury, Ken 120-121
Rhodes, Wilfred 67
Richards, Barry 109
Richardson, Arthur 115
Richardson, Victor 50, 55, 66, 196
Rigg, Keith 67, 196
Ring, Doug 196
Ringwood, John 159
Roberts, Brian 'Whale' 152
Robertson-Glasgow, R. C. 181
Robins, Walter 67, 139, 181
Robinson, Ray 196
Robinson, Ray (the writer) 112, 174, 181
Roebuck, Peter 181
Rosenwater, Irving 181
Rowan, Eric 202
Ruth, Babe 50, 113, 188
Ryder, Jack 35, 115, 117, 124-131, 133, 196

Saggers, Ron 126, 196
Sehwag, Virender 200, 201
Sievers, Morrie 196
Smith, Graham 116
Sobers, Garry 109, 156, 175
Statham, Brian 98
Stephens, Alf 21
Sutcliffe, Herbert 31, 66, 137, 199, 203
Swanton, E. W. 'Jim' 174
Sweet, Gary 108-109

Tallon, Don 109, 175, 196
Taylor, Mark 181
Tendulkar, Sachin 101, 109, 175, 181
Tennyson, Lord 162-163
Tests the Don 'won' 133-143
Thoms, George 128
Thomson, A. A. 174
Thomson, Jeff 120
Thorpe, Graham 204
Thurlow, H. M. 'Pud' 40, 106, 135, 196
Timms, Darryl 153-154
Toshack, Ernie 196
Tribe, George 126, 196
Trumper, Victor 161, 172, 200
Turner, C. T. B. 'Terror' 27
Tyson, Frank 175

Verity, Hedley 67
Vincent, Cyril 50
Voce, Bill 53, 56, 67, 106, 162

Waite, Merv 196
Walker, Alan 128
Wall, Tim 133, 195
Ward, Frank 67, 196
Warne, Shane 85, 101, 120, 175, 183
Warner, P. F. 'Plum' 46, 54, 55, 56
Waters, Leo 113
Watson, Billy 119-120
Watt, David 126
Waugh, Mark 202
Waugh, Steve 120, 166, 181, 183, 201
Webb, Syd 130
Whatman, George 20, 23
Whatman, Richard 20
White, J. C. 'Farmer' 37, 134
Whitelaw, Arthur 113
Whitington, R. S. 'Dick' 130, 162
Woodfull, Bill 55, 56, 106, 134, 137, 195, 204
  Unhappy at the Don 162
Worrell, Frank 169, 192
Wright, Doug 126, 141, 172

Yardley, Norman 80, 108, 143

Zaheer Abbas 202

In 1927-28 made a century in his first Shield match. In 1928-29 selected for Australia.

Next season he broke world record by scoring 452 not out for NSW against Queensland.

In 1930 he broke many records in England; scored 334 in a Test. In a Test in 1934 he made 304.

Operation for appendicitis at end of 1934 tour. Fit again he led Australia's 1936-37 team.

Bradman captained the Test team in England in 1938 and scored 13 centuries on tour.

When war came joined air force. Transferred to army. Discharged medically unfit with fibrositis.

He had a tough time with his health, but in 1946-47 again played for Australia. Although far below his best he made scores of 187 and 234 in Tests against England in Australia.

During 1947-48 season he scored his 100th century in fewer than 300 innings in first-class cricket.